LINCOLN AND THE PREACHERS

LINCOLN

And the Preachers

by

EDGAR DeWITT JONES

Author of *Lords of Speech* and
American Preachers of Today

WITH AN INTRODUCTION BY

WILLIAM H. TOWNSEND

Harper & Brothers Publishers

New York

LINCOLN AND THE PREACHERS

*

*

FIRST EDITION

K-X

THIS BOOK

IS GRATEFULLY AND AFFECTIONATELY

INSCRIBED TO

WILLIAM O. STODDARD, JR.,

Son of one of Mr. Lincoln's Secretaries

A LIVING LINK BETWEEN THE PRESENT

AND THE WAR YEARS 1861-65

My Friend and Mentor of Two Decades

CONTENTS

* * *

Introduction

Preacher Cartwright knew Abraham Lincoln; jogged the Methodist Circuit over the same roads the Springfield lawyer traveled to court; ran against him for Congress; sat anxiously at the trial table when Lincoln successfully defended his grandson charged with murder; wrote his memoirs of more than five hundred pages—and never mentioned Lincoln's name!

Preacher Gurley, Lincoln's pastor in Washington, stood beside him over the casket of his dead little boy; knelt with him on the rear porch of the White House while southwest winds brought to them the acrid smell of gunpowder from the distant cannon of Second Bull Run; kept the President's confidence about the Emancipation Proclamation—and left only a pitifully meager record of that intimate association!

Pondering all this, while turning the manuscript pages of the present volume, I could not escape the conviction that history would have been greatly enriched had Preacher Jones personally known Abraham Lincoln as did these two brethren of the cloth.

Early in his career as a minister, eager, alert Edgar DeWitt Jones, who went to college in the Bluegrass town where Mary Todd was born and reared, found the Lincoln trail. It began at Bloomington, Illinois—the little county seat with tree-skirted streets on a gentle hill that Lincoln loved; the scene of his celebrated "lost speech"; the home of Jesse W. Fell, his early presidential sponsor, and of David Davis and Leonard Swett, who swung the delegates to him at the Chicago convention. It was the place where a group of Lincoln's old friends still lived—where the people liked to talk of the tall, angular, homely lawyer who for many years sat around the courthouse, told stories, cracked jokes, played with their children, and then went away to fame and martyrdom in smoke and flags.

There was Judge Owen T. Reeves, who had tried cases with and against Lincoln; and "Private Joe" Fifer, an ex-Governor of Illinois, who had heard the "lost speech"; and James E. Ewing, son of the proprietor of the Old National Hotel, where Lincoln had stopped when he attended, twice each year, the sessions of the McLean circuit court. It was Ewing, youthful and but recently admitted to the bar, who had met the President-elect on the sidewalk in front of the courthouse on his last afternoon in Bloomington. Ewing was fond of relating that brief, unforgettable conversation.

"Well, you have gotten to be a lawyer," smilingly observed Lincoln as he shook hands with a warm clasp. "Let me give you some advice; don't meddle with politics; stick to the law."

"Mr. President," replied Ewing, "I fear your example may prove more alluring than your advice."

But Lincoln had ceased to smile. "No! No!" he said soberly, shaking his head. Then, as they passed through the arched doorway of the dingy little courthouse, he shook his head again. "That was an accident," he said reflectively.

For fourteen years, Edgar DeWitt Jones lived in daily association with men and women steeped in the Lincoln tradition, receiving them into the church, performing their marriage ceremonies, burying their dead, listening to their reminiscences, speaking at Lincoln exercises, writing articles, studying and collecting Lincoln books with unflagging interest and enthusiasm. Then he left Bloomington and took up his residence in the great industrial city of Detroit, where he became pastor of what is now one of the largest church congregations in the United States. Today his modest Lincoln shelves of the Bloomington years have expanded into an entire Lincoln Room, which any private collector would be proud to call his own.

More than a quarter of a century has passed since those golden years of youthful ministry, and world-wide honors have come to

Edgar DeWitt Jones from many sources. Recognized as one of the most eloquent orators of his day, he has filled pulpits in other lands, has represented his church as a delegate to various conferences abroad, and has served as president of his denomination's International Conference. In 1939, he won the W. J. Long prize for the best Lincoln sermon. This address, with its deep sincerity, modest dignity, and simple elegance of diction, will take its place among the truly great pulpit orations of all time. He is a member of the Advisory Group of the Lincoln Foundation and one of the directors of the Abraham Lincoln Association.

As work on the present volume neared completion, the author was loath to lay down his pen. A priceless, hitherto inaccessible source of Lincoln material remained to be explored. When on July 26, 1926, Robert Todd Lincoln, last surviving child of Abraham Lincoln, died, he left a strict interdict for twenty-one years upon the great collection of his father's private papers, which he had deposited some years before with the Library of Congress. To the "faithful," these years went by with leaden tread.

Finally there came a day that will live in history—July 25, 1947— the last day of the long interdict—a clear, starlit evening in Washington. From far and near the clan had gathered. The "yankees" were there from north and east of the Ohio River. The "rebels," faring better than their Civil War forebears, were there, too, from North Carolina, Tennessee, and Kentucky. Over in Whittal Pavilion of the Library of Congress, the genial librarian, Dr. Luther H. Evans, gave a dinner to a group of guests. As I stepped off the elevator, a tall, courtly, unmistakable figure was visible across the threshold of an open door—Edgar DeWitt Jones was already deep in the fellowship of this memorable occasion.

Two hours later, one minute past midnight, Dr. Percy Powell twirled the dials of massive safes, and wide swinging doors, amidst the popping of flashlights and whirr of motion picture cameras, revealed the long-awaited treasure. I shall always hold in memory a vignette of Edgar Jones as dawn crept through the Library windows: broad shoulders, bent slightly from fatigue—beads of perspiration glistening on ruddy brow—a drawer of cards from the huge index cabinet on a table—eyes squinting under the glare of many lamps— a long, unlighted cigar chewed gently, meditatively. Here, indeed, a scholar was at work! And this book received its finishing touches.

Dr. Jones has followed the Lincoln trail for so many years that I was not surprised to hear him say on one occasion that he has often dreamed of Lincoln. One of these dreams was so amusing that I should like to record it here in Dr. Jones' own words:

"I dreamed I went to the bank in Detroit where I do my business, sat down at a vice-president's desk and told him I wished to make a loan. I stated the sum, which was considerably larger than any loan I had negotiated hitherto. The banker said, 'We have been making you loans on your own name, but for this sum we'd appreciate your giving us another name.' 'That is all right,' I replied. 'Whose name would you like?' 'Well now,' the banker answered, 'how about Abraham Lincoln—he appears to be a friend of yours?' I said that that was agreeable to me, and I accordingly set out for Springfield, though I have no recollection of the actual trip. Upon arriving there I sought out the law office of 'Lincoln and Herndon.' I went up the stairs and found Mr. Lincoln in his plain office engaged in looking over some papers. He greeted me cordially and asked what he could do for me. I told him, and he said, 'Let me have the note.' I handed it to him—and just then I woke up!"

If only that dream had lasted at least one minute longer, we would have known whether or not his credit was good with Abraham Lincoln!

In *Lincoln and the Preachers*, Dr. Jones has treated his subject, as the title indicates, from an informal, exclusively personal viewpoint. He does not press upon the reader any oracular theory about Lincoln's soul or his religion or lack of it. No citadels of reason are stormed or besieged. There is no wrestling with constitutional questions, no delving into the mighty problems of state which sorely perplexed the President, no discussion of military strategy, no description of gory battles. The author is completely absorbed in the task of making his readers see Abraham Lincoln, *the man*, and the clergymen who were his contemporaries, and in many instances his friends and advisers— fresh furrows in a rich but neglected corner of a much-plowed field.

It seems to me that Dr. Jones has accomplished his purpose to a degree, perhaps, beyond his fondest hope. He has written a book unique in the annals of Lincolniana.

WILLIAM H. TOWNSEND

28 Mentelle Park
Lexington, Kentucky

Acknowledgments

The author wishes to express his appreciation to the individuals, libraries, publishers and groups listed below for their kindness in rendering the following services and permissions:

The Library of Congress for courteous and prompt compliance with requests for photostats of manuscripts and valuable information.

The Detroit Public Library for generous help in supplying books and pamphlets, particularly rare Lincoln sermonic material.

The Illinois State Historical Society and the Abraham Lincoln Association for important data.

Mr. William H. Townsend, of Lexington, Kentucky, for his gracious Introduction to the book, and for delightful hours with him amidst his Lincoln books, pictures, and documents.

The following fellow-Lincolnians for suggestions and advice: Carl Sandburg, James G. Randall, Louis A. Warren, Paul M. Angle, Lloyd Lewis, Harry E. Pratt, Wayne C. Townley, Joseph Fort Newton, W. O. Stoddard, Jr., Thomas Irving Starr, Rufus Rockwell Wilson, and Herbert W. Fay.

Mr. Kenneth W. Greenawalt, of New York, for supplying a copy of the Henry Ward Beecher Sermon of Sunday, February 26, 1860, and Plymouth Church, Brooklyn, New York, for permission to reproduce it here, along with the photograph of Dr. Beecher.

Dr. Perry Epler Gresham, my devoted friend and successor at Central Woodward Church, Detroit, for a painstaking scrutiny of the completed manuscript.

The Rev. Melville Brooks Gurley, of Cynwyd, Pennsylvania, for the photograph of his grandfather, the Rev. Dr. Phineas D. Gurley. The Methodist Information for the photograph of Bishop Simpson.

Abraham Lincoln Quarterly for permission to reproduce the letter to Allen N. Ford.

Farrar & Rinehart, Inc., New York, for permission to quote a paragraph from Edgar Lee Master's *The Sangamon*.

Houghton Mifflin Company, Boston, for permission to quote a quatrain from John Drinkwater's impressive play *Abraham Lincoln*.

The Macmillan Company, New York, for permission to use two stanzas from Vachel Lindsay's "Abraham Lincoln Walks at Midnight in Springfield, Illinois."

The Rev. Charles A. Tupper for highly prized research in and about Springfield Illinois.

Mr. Irving I. Katz, historian, for vital facts pertaining to Lincoln and the Jews.

Mrs. William Clark for painstaking secretarial work done with a contagious cheerfulness.

Finally, to my own Lincoln Library for fruitful years of inspiration and a mine of information not yet fully explored.

E. DeW. J.

LINCOLN AND THE PREACHERS

Chapter I

I Have Lived with Lincoln

"Never a moment was he found unlovable or vain."

****

THIS is a book about Abraham Lincoln and the spiritual leaders of his day who for one reason or another entered into his life. The pages that follow are peopled by circuit riders, revivalists, rural and city pastors, doctors of divinity, together with a smaller number of prelates, priests, and rabbis, whose presence contribute a spirit of catholicity to the story. What about these gentlemen of the cloth who were friends, acquaintances, and in some instances, counselors of Lincoln? Of what stature were they, and how did these men impress and influence the "prairie lawyer" and later President of the United States? Here is an attempt to answer these questions, and to portray the character of some of these prophets of the Most High who were big men in their own right.

To the extent of my familiarity with Lincoln literature I do not find that this kind of book has been written up to now. A field of unexplored Lincolniana has both novelty and charm, and I confess a sensitivity and responsiveness to both. One must invade a controversial realm of the Lincoln saga, namely, his religious or perhaps more accurately his theological views. However, the contents of the chapters which follow are not, I hold, controversial, save to those who come to the pages with preconceived notions or dogmatic opinions for or against Mr. Lincoln as a man of a religious faith which grew with the years.

On the one hand, there are those who think or write of Lincoln as "a man of God," and on the other, a steadily decreasing number who label him as a "freethinker," "agnostic," or "unbeliever." Students of this famed American President are for the most part aware of the fact that during the past thirty or forty years the basis of this religious issue has shifted from what contemporaries said about Mr. Lincoln's religious faith, or unfaith, to the surer ground of what he himself said and wrote about the Bible, prayer, and immortality, buttressed by the greatening of his spiritual life during the war years at Washington. Thus Lord Charnwood in commenting on the "Second Inaugural" writes: "He [Lincoln] could wield like no other modern writer the language of the Prayer Book, so he could speak of prayer without the smallest embarrassment in talk with a general or statesman. It is possible that this was a development of later years."

I

The caption of this chapter, "I Have Lived with Lincoln," may appear presumptuous to some. Still, I think there is a justification for it. In the home of my childhood there was a copy of *The Life, Speeches, and Public Services of Abraham Lincoln*, by J. H. Barrett, a big book of more than eight hundred pages. It was not attractively bound, and other than a steel engraving frontispiece of Mr. Lincoln, there were only a few illustrations: woodcuts of the Springfield residence, the site of the birthplace in Kentucky, and the Anderson Creek Ferry where the boy Lincoln had served for some nine months; these, and perhaps a few others; yet this book strangely fascinated me, and I pored over its pages at a time when *Robinson Crusoe* and the *Swiss Family Robinson* competed for my interest. To be sure, I never read the book from cover to cover in those days—that was too much of an ordeal for an eight-year-old boy; but I reread many times the opening chapter with its account of Lincoln's boyhood; and the last chapter in this book held me under a spell—the chapter which described the firing of another shot "heard around the world"—a shot that stilled forever a great and gentle heart!

In 1906, after brief pastorates in Kentucky and Ohio, I became minister of First Christian Church, Bloomington, Illinois, where I was to reside for fourteen rememberable years. Bloomington, county seat of McLean County, was part of the Old Eighth Judicial District over which Mr. Lincoln and his associates regularly traveled; also, this inland city was the home of David Davis, and for a time of Leonard Swett, two of the three men accredited with making Mr. Lincoln the nominee of the Republican party in 1860. The third member of this illustrious trio, Jesse W. Fell, resided in the town of Normal which adjoins Bloomington on the north. The memory of Mr. Fell is fragrant to this day in Bloomington and Normal. Furthermore, Mr. Lincoln had many other friends in Bloomington, and it was in this county seat town that he made important speeches in 1856 and 1858 —speeches that helped shape the speaker's political destiny. Moreover, when I became a citizen of Bloomington the centenary of Lincoln's birth was only three years ahead. A myriad newspaper and magazine articles, as well as scores of books with the Emancipator as theme were in the making, or had already appeared. Also at that time Bloomington boasted of six eminent men who had known Lincoln, lawyers all, who were still living and conspicuous in city and state affairs. Five of these men had been young attorneys when Mr. Lincoln rode the circuit and mingled freely with his fellow lawyers. The most widely known of this group was former Vice-President of the United States, Adlai E. Stevenson, born in Christian County, Kentucky. He came to Illinois as a young man, and first heard Lincoln speak in 1852, and also in the notable Lincoln-Douglas debates of 1858. Mr. Stevenson was a gentleman of the old school of statesmen, courtly, tall and lean of flank; a raconteur of parts, and a delightful host.

Next to Mr. Stevenson in public affairs was his former law partner,

James S. Ewing, a man of distinguished appearance, who had been Mr. Cleveland's minister to Belgium in that President's second administration. It was my good fortune to hear Mr. Ewing's impressive address at the banquet of the Illinois Schoolmasters' Club, February 12, 1909, a speech which appears unabridged in a book published in Bloomington in 1910, entitled *Abraham Lincoln by Some Men Who Knew Him*, and now a rarity. Another of this group who knew Lincoln was Judge Reuben M. Benjamin. He, too, heard Lincoln's speeches on May 26, 1856 and on September 4, 1858. Judge Benjamin was of Quaker stock, a man of moral as well as of legal substance. Also, there was Judge Owen T. Reeves, a jurist of ability, and for many years dean of the Bloomington Law School; a veteran of the Civil War, he attained the rank of colonel. Isaac N. Phillips, for sixteen years reporter of the Supreme Court of Illinois, and a Lincoln orator of superior eloquence, author of *Lincoln* and other books, likewise adorned this circle. Last, and certainly not least, was the Honorable Joseph W. Fifer, a private in the Civil War, and governor of Illinois from 1888 to 1892. Fifer's recollection of Lincoln's Bloomington speech of 1856 was unsurpassed by any other account to which I had listened on the same fascinating theme. To the end of his long life "Private Joe's" mind was clear, although he was blind for a decade.

I came to know these men as friends and neighbors, I heard them talk of Lincoln for hours informally, and I listened to the public addresses of Stevenson, Ewing, Phillips, and Fifer, with unalloyed pleasure. On my shelves are the books of three of this enchanting coterie, characteristically autographed. It was when I "loafed" with these men and "invited my soul" that I really began to live with Lincoln.

When I entered on my Bloomington ministry I was privileged to have as a member of the congregation a woman of remarkable personality, Mrs. Judith Ann Bradner. She was then in her early nineties, a lady of quality, with traces of girlish beauty still discernible in her person. She was a daughter of William T. Major who came to Bloomington from Bourbon County, Kentucky, and soon was numbered among the leading citizens of the community. Mrs. Bradner knew Lincoln, not in a formal or official way, but as one of her dearest friends. Always when the Springfield lawyer visited Bloomington, unless unforseen events prevented, he called to see Mrs. Bradner (Mrs. Edward Allin was her name then). Sometimes Mr. Lincoln was accompanied by his lawyer friend, Leonard Swett; oftener he came alone. Mrs. Bradner was present at social affairs where Mr. Lincoln and sometimes Stephen A. Douglas were guests. Often she danced the Virginia reel and other square dances with Mr. Lincoln. Once I asked her what kind of a dancing partner he was. She smiled and shook the corkscrew curls that fell about her forehead as she replied: "Mr. Lincoln wasn't what you would call a graceful man on the floor, but when he took my arm I knew a real man had hold of me."

Also in my Bloomington congregation was one of the gentlest and most guileless of men I have known, Francis Marion Emerson. The only time I recall when he spunked up was when I announced in 1909 that my next Sunday morning sermon would be on "The Religion of Abraham Lincoln." Now Mr. Emerson had been a Douglas Democrat, and had met Lincoln only once or twice. After the benediction that Sunday this usually placid man waited to see me. There was a gleam in his eyes. "So you are goin' to preach on Abe Lincoln's religion next Sunday?" I nodded my head in affirmation. "I'll be out to hear you! I never knew Abe had any religion worth preaching about." So that was that!

There was another link with the Lincoln years in that congregation. On October 19, 1908, I united in marriage Mrs. Sarah Swayne, the widowed daughter of David Davis, to Mr. John T. Lillard, a leading lawyer of Bloomington, and later received her into the membership of First Christian Church. She was large of frame, a woman of impressive presence, widely traveled, and I recall she spoke French fluently and was well acquainted with French literature. Many an evening I sat in the library of her home where a large portrait of her famous father adorned one wall, and another of Abraham Lincoln, the man Mr. Davis helped to nominate for the Presidency, graced the opposite wall.

Also among my Bloomington friends who had known or heard Lincoln was Captain John H. Burnham, one of the founders of the Illinois Historical Society. The Captain and I were fellow members of the College Alumni Association of Bloomington, and I often had him for a seat-mate at the dinners. He was a fluent conversationalist, and historically minded. On May 19, 1860, the day after Mr. Lincoln was nominated for the Presidency at Chicago, Captain Burnham wrote a letter to his father in Massachusetts. He told of having attended a meeting where Mr. Lincoln had been announced to lecture on "Inventions," but that the lecture never came off. Here follow two paragraphs from the letter:

> I have seen Lincoln several times, and heard him speak once. His popularity as a speaker consists in joking and story telling, and I have heard many better orators. I heard him a year ago in a law case. In the evening he was advertised to lecture on "Inventions" for the benefit of the Ladies Literary Association, admittance 25 cts.

> I paid a quarter and went early to get a seat. It was a beautiful evening and the lecture had been well advertised, but for some reason not yet explained, only 40 persons were present, and old Abe would not speak to such a small crowd, and they paid us back our quarters at the door.

It was during the Bloomington years that I came to know Vachel Lindsay, the Springfield poet whose poem entitled "Abraham Lincoln Walks at Midnight in Springfield, Illinois," rates him among the few who wrote truly great poems on the most written about of our Presidents. From 1910 until his untimely death in 1931, I rejoiced in Vachel's friendship. A copy of his poem done in his artistic script, and inscribed to me, occupies a conspicuous place on the walls of

my Lincoln Room. This poem which I have recited in public addresses above two hundred times ranks in my opinion with Edwin
Markham's "Lincoln" and Walt Whitman's "O My Captain! My
Captain!" as one of the three noblest tributes to "the prairie-lawyer,
master of us all." How solemnly impressive are the opening stanzas:

> It is portentous and a thing of state
> That here at midnight in our little town
> A mourning figure walks and will not rest,
> Near the old court-house pacing up and down,
>
> Or by his homestead, or in shadowed yards
> He lingers where his children used to play,
> Or through the market, on well-worn stones
> He stalks until the dawn-stars burn away.[1]

In those Bloomington years, and especially during and after the
centennial celebration of Lincoln's birth, the spell of the Uncommon
Commoner seemed to rest upon me and to hold me fast. How often
he had walked these familiar streets "as in times before"! Bronzed
markers served to remind me of his "last speech" delivered in Major's
Hall; at the courthouse square where in the "temple of justice" long
since torn down and replaced with a spacious new structure, he had
argued cases, and where on a memorable day he wrote for Jesse W.
Fell his famous "Autobiography." I thought of Lincoln walking
those Bloomington streets, not at midnight, but in broad daylight,
little dreaming what history had in store for him.

II

In 1920 we said "good-by" to Bloomington and came to Detroit
to build a metropolitan church. It was a long pull and a hard one,
but in October, 1928, that edifice was dedicated. In the stately Gothic

[1] "Abraham Lincoln Walks at Midnight in Springfield, Illinois," from *The
Congo*, by Vachel Lindsay. Copyright, 1914, by The Macmillan Company; re-
newal, 1942, by Elizabeth C. Lindsay.

structure which by the help of the Lord and a large congregation I was permitted to build, an impressive Lincoln window looks out upon the congregation from the north transept. It was designed by the late H. Kay Herbert, and portrays the Emancipator in the act of striking the shackles from a slave boy. The cost was three thousand dollars which I raised by popular subscription among friends in and outside the church, and from others scattered throughout as many perhaps as a dozen states. This window was dedicated in 1930 by Dr. William E. Barton with a noble address and impressive ceremonies.

During these Detroit years I have companied with a growing collection of Lincoln books and pictures. There are larger and more costly private libraries of Lincoln lore than mine, but I doubt if any of these has brought the owner more satisfaction than mine has to me. It numbers about six hundred items, volumes, pictures, monographs, including some rarities. Many of my more recent purchases are inscribed, and my files of letters from Lincoln authors and others interested in the subject are a source of delight. My Lincoln Room is filled to overflowing with treasures, and my shelves grow apace.

I have lived intimately not only with Lincoln books but also with many of the Lincoln authors and collectors, a galaxy of shining names, including: Carl Sandburg, Judge James W. Bollinger, Paul M. Angle, William H. Townsend, Joseph Fort Newton, Harry E. Pratt, Louis A. Warren, Otto Eisenschmil, William O. Stoddard, Jr., son of one of Mr. Lincoln's secretaries, Thomas Irving Starr, and George A. Dondero. Then too, I have more than a passing acquaintance with James G. Randall, W. E. Baringer, and Roy P. Basler. I know Jay Monaghan, and have shaken the hand of Lauriston Bullard. Some of the great I knew have passed from this earthly scene; for instance, Ida M. Tarbell, who stood with me before the glorious Lincoln window in Central Woodward Church, as one at prayer. Gone from the earthly scene are Beverly W. Howe and Clint Clay Tilton, leaving lonesome places against my sky. Nor would I omit the venerable Herbert W. Fay, guardian of the Lincoln Tomb, Springfield, nor J. Henri Ripstra, Ralph G. Lindstrom, Rufus Rockwell Wilson, President Kincaid of Lincoln Memorial University, nor Stewart McClelland, his predecessor there, and Gerald McMurtry, Lincoln professor in the same institution. But time and space would fail me if I wrote here the names of others I have met along the Lincoln trail and was thereby both gentled and inspired.

I was privileged to know Governor Henry Horner, twice elected chief executive of his state. Twice I was a guest of this able statesman and loyal follower of the Lincoln trail. At the Governor's mansion I looked over his large and valuable collection of Lincoln books with my host as mentor and guide—an evening indelibly graven on my memory. New Salem was at that time in process of reconstruction, and Governor Horner sent me to inspect that village on the Sangamon with the supervising architect as guide.

I make it a point when I am in Springfield, Illinois, to visit the Lincoln Tomb and Monument. I do not know how many times I have been at Oak Ridge Cemetery where reposes not only all that is mortal of Abraham Lincoln, but also the earthly tenement of his law partner and embattled biographer, William H. Herndon. The grave of the Rev. Charles Dresser, the Episcopal clergyman who performed the wedding ceremony for Mr. Lincoln and Mary Todd, November 4, 1842, is on a hill not far from the Tomb. Likewise, it is in Oak Ridge that Vachel Lindsay is buried.

The Lincoln Tomb and Monument is not remarkable for its design or artistry, but no matter, the world would beat a path to that place even though but the plainest stone marked it. Since it was rehabilitated and refurbished some seventeen years ago, the Tomb and Monument—they are really one and the same—has a much more pleasing and impressive effect than before. To those of us who know him, the venerable custodian of the Tomb is second in interest only to the shrine itself. Herbert W. Fay was born in DeKalb County, Illinois, way back in 1859. He came to the Tomb as custodian in 1921, and to the day this is written, which is the Year of Our Lord

1947, and the month of December, Mr. Fay has rainbowed his duties with an interest in and an affection for the memory of Lincoln that is touching and beautiful. For this man's interest in Lincoln began when he was a little boy. He remembers the shock that shook the nation when the news of the assassination blanketed the nation in gloom and sadness.

Herbert W. Fay's collection of Lincolniana is prodigious, numbering, so one writer says, over one million items, and valued at $250,000. These, or more accurately the most important items, he loves to show to visitors who are interested and will listen patiently to his story of how he procured them, and why they are so precious. Mr. Fay estimates that more than three million persons from all the corners of the earth have visited the Tomb since he became its custodian. Daily he takes groups of from ten to forty at a time through his lecture, which abounds in dramatic incidents and relates the attempts to steal the body, and the final entombment, which put an end to the fiendish designs of those who would violate a grave or tomb. It takes Mr. Fay some twenty minutes to do justice to his lecture and answer myriad questions—sometimes longer.

The hosts who pilgrimage to the Tomb include the great and the humble; the proud and the pitiful; the rich and the poor. Many who have stood at this shrine made history and world-wide headlines in the news—Lloyd George when he was prime minister of Great Britain; Clemenceau, "the Tiger of France"; beautiful Queen Marie of Rumania; Eduard Benes of Czechoslovakia; Calvin Coolidge; Herbert Hoover; and Franklin D. Roosevelt.

The Tomb has been visited at least once, Mr. Fay says, by every President of the United States who followed Lincoln, save only Warren G. Harding, and he had made plans to stop off in Springfield on his return from the West Coast when death unexpectedly intervened.

Now all this is preliminary to an account of my first visit to the Tomb after its reconstruction, and indeed only a few weeks following President Herbert Hoover's dedicatory address. I came into the Rotunda to find Mr. Fay in the midst of his lecture to a group of some twenty visitors. It was a cosmopolitan company, and included two elderly gentlemen who appeared to be visitors from southern Europe, three or four farmers, their wives and children, a businessman or two, half a dozen schoolteachers, and several half-grown boys and girls. The custodian had reached a dramatic place in his narrative, describing the sinking of the coffin in solid concrete. "It lies just here," he explained, pointing down . . . Just here I came in!

Mr. Fay saw me, bowed with old-world courtesy, and breaking off his lecture, turned to his listeners and said this thing which quite caught me off guard: "Ladies and gentlemen, my friend, Dr. Jones of Detroit, a Lincoln orator, has just come in, and from now on he will talk to you about Lincoln and this tomb."

Now I could no more take on from where the custodian left off, than I can do any other thing for which I am not prepared. I had a pretty fair idea of the history of the Tomb, but not sufficient to substitute on short notice for Mr. Fay. What did I do? I fell back on poetry. I decided to quote a famous Lincoln poem. My disposition when called unexpectedly to speak on public occasions has been: "When in doubt quote poetry." So I said something like this:

"Mr. Fay and visitors, I am appreciative of the honor the custodian does me when he asks me to complete his lecture, but no one could do that as Mr. Fay alone can do it. However, since he has asked me to speak, I will simply recite for you a famous Lincoln sonnet entitled "The Cenotaph," by James T. MacKay . . .

> And so they buried Lincoln? Strange and vain!
> Has any creature thought of Lincoln hid
> In any vault, 'neath any coffin lid,
> In all the years since that wild spring of pain?
> 'Tis false,—he never in the grave hath lain.
> You could not bury him although you slid
> Upon his clay the Cheops Pyramid

Or heaped it with the Rocky Mountain chain.
They slew themselves; they but set Lincoln free.
In all this earth his great heart beats as strong,
Shall beat while pulses throb to chivalry
And burn with hate of tyranny and wrong.
Whoever will may find him, anywhere
Save in the tomb. Not there, he is not there!

Then I bowed myself out and went about some business I had in the city.

III

For thirty-eight years I have been speaking on the Lincoln theme, above a thousand times in all, and in Detroit and Michigan some four hundred times. At the church in Detroit which I had the honor to serve for over a quarter of a century, I inaugurated the Annual Lincoln Dinner, to which came as orators of the occasion Sandburg, Angle, Newton, Dondero, Stoddard, Warren, and many others, and, although I am emeritus now of this good church, I am by request of my successor, still lord of this Lincoln event. In Glasgow, Scotland, I spoke on Lincoln to a capacity audience in old Renfield Street Free Church following the usual evening preaching service. At the close the people were slow to leave the building, and I met a goodly group of Scotsmen who wanted to ask me about certain facts of the Commoner's life. In 1935, on the Italian Steamship *Rex*, I had Lincoln for theme as I talked to a group of fellow voyagers. Once on a February Sunday morning I faced a thousand inmates of the Southern Michigan Prison for audience as I traced the story of the long hard climb of the Kentucky-born hero to his place among the stars; and more attentive auditors I do not recall than these men behind prison walls.

Everywhere it was the same. The Lincoln theme is of endless interest to all kinds and conditions of men, women, and children.

Drinkwater, who knew his Lincoln, explained the perennial interest in the Lincoln saga:

> When the high heart we magnify
> And the sure vision celebrate,
> And worship greatness passing by,
> Ourselves are great.[2]

IV

It has been my good fortune to "sit in" on many Lincoln events of historic interest, and none more impressive or so exciting as the opening of the Robert Todd Lincoln papers, on July 26, 1947. Thirty-two of us sat down in the Congressional Library to a dinner on the evening of the 25th, guests of librarian Dr. Luther H. Evans. The "great" of Lincolniana were there, biographers, collectors, students, with Randall, Sandburg, Warren, Angle, Bullard, Basler, Wilson, and other top-flight authors present. After the excellent dinner the next four hours were spent in listening to speeches, most of them brief but fascinating.

Carl Sandburg led off with a story or two, then picked up his faithful guitar and sang several songs of the Lincoln period. William H. Townsend of Lexington, Kentucky, followed with a tribute to Robert Todd Lincoln, with whom he had perhaps a more intimate acquaintance than any other of the men present. He told some incidents of Robert Lincoln's kindnesses which that reticent gentleman never would permit to be told in his lifetime—acts of beneficence which mirrored the heart of a man sometimes called cold and aloof. The white-haired Rufus Rockwell Wilson recited James Whitcomb Riley's "The Old Man and Jim," which he said was held in high esteem by James Russell Lowell. Practically all who spoke while eagerly awaiting the opening of the huge safe which contained the papers said that they expected nothing sensational or spectacular,

[2] From *Abraham Lincoln*, by John Drinkwater. Copyright, 1927, by Houghton Mifflin Company.

although they were agreed that the items would be of priceless value to authors and Lincoln students everywhere.

By and by they called on me. For a wonder, I was strangely inarticulate, and responded in a single sentence: "The three great events of my life have been my marriage, the delivery of my church from debt, and this gathering of Lincolnians."

When I sat down one of my friends asked me why I hadn't "let myself go." I replied by relating a story so old it was new to him: John Johnson, hero of the Johnstown flood, died and went to heaven. No sooner did he arrive, than he gathered about him a crowd of celestial citizens and thus spoke to them: "I am John Johnson, hero of the Johnstown flood. When the big dam broke, I mounted a horse and raced down the valley crying, 'The dam has broke, run for your lives!' Oh, I tell you, that was a flood, a terrible flood." Each time Johnson spoke, he noticed a little old man in the crowd sniff and walk away in disgust. At last Johnson took one of his hearers aside and inquired: "Who is that little old man who when I tell my story of the Johnstown flood sniffs and walks out on me?" The heavenly citizen looked surprised, "Why sir!" he said, "don't you know? That's NOAH!"

No, there were at least fourteen "Noahs" in the group about that table, and I knew it.

I trust I am not presumptuous in saying that in a spiritual sense I have lived with the immortal Lincoln for some forty years, and that, patient reader, is why the curtain is about to rise on *Lincoln and the Preachers.*

Chapter II

Some Pioneer Preachers Lincoln Knew

"Not the cushion, and the slipper, not the peaceful and the studious;
Pioneers! O Pioneers!"

****

THE pioneer preachers of the Middle West were a forthright, fearless and sacrificial host. They were certainly not in the business of preaching for mercenary reasons. For the most part in those early days they received little else but their board and some gifts of various natures, wearing apparel or produce, but little or no money, whether as itinerant revivalists or settled pastors. For years the latter were not numerous. These frontier heralds of the Cross combined with their preaching, farming, merchandising, carpentering, and, in some instances, the sale of Bibles and subscription books.

Sherwood Eddy in his *The Kingdom of God and the American Dream* says: "Lincoln never came under the influence of a single intelligent spiritual minister during his early life. The crude Kentucky Baptists of the period often ranted against Sunday schools, Bible, Missionary and 'track' societies. Many a thoughtful man revolting against such preaching as Lincoln heard in his youth became an infidel."

There is truth in this statement, but not all the truth. Many of these pioneer proclaimers of the Word were, it is true, illiterate, but not all of them were unintelligent. Then too, for the larger part their hearers were illiterate but not unintelligent. It took not only brawn but brains as well to conquer the wilderness. Along about the 1840's college-trained ministers with academic degrees invaded Illinois, where they established both churches and colleges, often against heavy odds.

"The clergymen of a century ago," writes Dr. Louis A. Warren, an authority on the parentage and childhood of Lincoln, "exerted a tremendous influence over the lives of American youth. With the earliest developments of the social instinct as the infant emerged into childhood, until the minister was called upon to preside over the rites of matrimony, he was as close to the family unit as the physician. The clergymen of that day were also the chief contributors to literature, which was predominantly of a religious nature, and their supervision of education also influenced the character of the school textbooks."

The name of the Rev. Jesse Head deserves first mention here simply because he officiated at the wedding of Nancy Hanks and Thomas Lincoln, June 12, 1806, in Washington County, Kentucky. Mr. Head was a Methodist, born in Maryland, son of William Edward Head. He married Jane Ramsey, daughter of Robert Ramsey, January 7, 1789, and probably came to Washington County, Kentucky, prior to 1797. He was a cabinet maker and justice of the peace, and was licensed or ordained a Methodist preacher in 1805. Politically, he was a Democrat, and an ardent admirer of Andrew Jackson. He also edited a local newspaper and was a useful citizen in many other ways.

There is no evidence that this pioneer Methodist ever saw the famed son of the couple he married that June day in 1806, nor is it clear that he had any influence over Thomas Lincoln in shaping his antislavery views, since Head himself, so the record shows, owned a few slaves. Jesse Head lived in the neighborhood and may have been acquainted with the young couple who sought him out to be married. He comes abruptly into the picture and as quickly drops out.

Nevertheless, he lives in the Lincoln saga because of that simple backwoods ceremony. Otherwise, it is likely his name would have had only a local significance.

William Downs, pioneer Baptist minister, was probably the first preacher that Abraham Lincoln ever heard. There is ground for this supposition. Downs preached at the Little Mount Church, which was formed shortly after Abraham Lincoln's birth, and is believed to be the church to which the Lincolns belonged. In 1816, Downs officiated at the wedding of Caleb Hazel and Mary Stevens, with Thomas Lincoln signing the groom's bond. Hazel was Abraham's schoolteacher and nearest neighbor of the Lincolns.

It is interesting to speculate whether when William Downs was in the midst of an oratorical flight he ever noticed a little dark-haired boy with eager eyes occupying a rude bench where he sat alongside his mother.

I

One of the first preachers Lincoln met and heard was the Rev. David Elkins who preached Nancy Hanks Lincoln's funeral sermon several months after her untimely death. Lincoln was nine years old at the time, and it is unlikely that he ever wholly forgot Preacher Elkins or what he said at her grave. Not much is known about this Baptist preacher who rates a paragraph or two from practically all Lincoln biographers. He was born in South Carolina, and served as a private in the Second South Carolina Militia in the War of 1812.

Parson Elkins was minister of the Rock Lick Baptist Church, and later of the Spice Valley Baptist Church, Spencer County, and in the 'forties removed to Lawrence County, dying in 1857. Spencer, in his *History of Kentucky Baptists*, says of Elkins: "He was a man of extraordinary natural intellect, but was uncultivated, being barely able to read. He was extremely poor as to this world's goods; and what was more, he was very indolent and slovenly in dress; yet it pleased the Lord to use him to good account, especially in his early days of his ministry. . . . His reputation was somewhat sullied in his later years, perhaps from too free use of strong drink."

Just what impression Elkins made on the boy Lincoln we do not know, but in view of the occasion, it is likely that Abraham paid little attention to the minister's shabby attire, which was probably as good as that of many of the men who stood about the grave that day. It would be strange, too, if Preacher Elkins failed to notice the motherless boy and to speak words of comfort and encouragement to him. It is probable that Elkins was a guest on that occasion in the humble grief-stricken home of the Lincolns, and that beneath that roof he lifted up his voice in prayer before the Indiana pioneer family fell asleep.

It was in the Indiana years that the Little Pigeon Creek Baptist Church came powerfully into the life of the Lincolns. That church was to this family and the neighbors as the shelter of a great rock in times of storm. Thomas Lincoln helped to build the meetinghouse, which was erected in 1820, and tradition has it that young Abraham assisted the carpenters. He was eleven years old at the time, and according to local records helped to fell the trees from which the lumber was made that went into the structure. A description of this famous little Baptist church has been preserved:

> The church, which stood one mile west of what is now Lincoln City, was built of logs, with a stick and mud chimney. It was a long, narrow building one and a half stories high, having a very large fireplace on one side of the building, with a pulpit made of roughly hewn boards. It had a window (with no glass, but heavy wooden shutters immediately behind it) at one end of the structure, and a ladder leading to the upper story where the people who came great distances might stay over night. Split logs, with wooden pegs for legs, and a puncheon floor, were also features of this church, the logs of which were sold and used in the building of a barn.

The stouthearted ministers who preached the gospel from the pulpit of that humble meetinghouse were a militant host, not of course in point of numbers, although there were at least twenty-five of these shepherds of souls whose names are known. It was because of their zeal, courage, perseverance and sacrificial devotion to the Cause that they stand out in the shining armor of the Lord. The names of eight of these men, together with some references to the manner of men they were, appear in a monograph on *Hoosier Preachers Lincoln Heard* by Dr. Louis A. Warren.

Doctrinally speaking, Jeremiah Cash, formerly of the Lincoln community in Kentucky, was possibly the most vigorous exponent heard at Little Pigeon Creek Church. At one of the sessions of the Association of Churches which met at that church in September 1829, where Lincoln may have been present, Cash became greatly offended and withdrew. Some unidentified individual had stated after one of the sessions that Cash believed "the doctrine of Predestination came from Hell and would go there and all who preached it." This incident reveals that not all the Baptists of this period and section were Calvinists in theology, although most of them probably were stoutly such. It also suggests that Jeremiah Cash was an independent thinker and a spirited person.

Such were Abraham Lincoln's religious surroundings in the Indiana years. It interests us to know that it was said by the children who grew up with him that he would go to church on Sunday morning, hear the sermon, and then come home and preach the same sermon better than the preacher. No one can evaluate adequately the influence of these sermons on slavery, temperance, and doctrinal subjects which Lincoln not only heard, but often repeated. Such teaching, vigorously presented, passed like the iron atoms of the blood into his being, and on such hidden resources he freely and fruitfully drew in the fateful years ahead.

In New Salem days Lincoln must have attended services at Concord Church, which was not far away and was of the Cumberland Presbyterian persuasion. The preacher at this church was often John McCutcheon Berry, a sturdy pioneer, born in Virginia, who served in the War of 1812, and was the father of the senior partner of "Berry and Lincoln," New Salem storekeepers. The story that his son drank himself out of this partnership has been shown by recent investigation to be erroneous.

Henry Onstot, proprietor of a tavern in New Salem, described "Old John Berry" as "the noblest Roman of them all; and like Paul among the prophets, stood head and shoulders above his brethren." (Here Onstot confused Saul, first King of Israel, with Paul the Apostle, but his point is still good.) Lincoln must have been well acquainted with the Rev. John M. Berry, and heard him preach many times. It is known that he thought highly of this sturdy pioneer who, to quote Onstot again, "did as much to civilize and Christianize the central of Illinois as any living man."

Another preacher at Concord Church was Abraham Goodpasture, who left a memory fragrant of good deeds and an amiable disposition. He was more broadminded than many of his contemporary proclaimers of the gospel, and had many loyal supporters.

Edgar Lee Masters in his book entitled *The Sangamon* gives an interesting and pathetic description of the passing of the Concord Meetinghouse where "Abe Lincoln of Illinois" was often an attendant. The literary skill of this Illinois novelist, biographer, and poet is nowhere more beautiful or more tenderly nostalgic than in the long lovely paragraph which follows:

> The church had two entrances, one for women and children and one for men. Later these entrances were reduced to one. A cupola was added to the roof. It was modernized, its old charm was taken away. Then it began to lean, and a large tree at the west grew through the wall and the roof. Rain poured into the room, the paper on the wall peeled off, the chandeliers were full of sticks and straw where the swallows had built their nests; the seats fell over or were twisted out of their place, the pulpit lay on the floor, having toppled, or been pushed from the rostrum, hymn books and small Bibles lay scattered in the aisles, vents in the roof showed the blue sky, or the stars by night.

Concord Church became a ruin, standing in the silence of the prairie. I believe no mischief attended it, that only abandonment brought its doors to flopping in the wind, and gave over its cushions on the floor to the minks and the rabbits. It was not a place for tramps, for tramps could find no object in wandering in that neighborhood. It stood at least as solitary, as silent, as uncomplaining as the stones in the church-yard, with the solemn oak trees in front of it and the prairie to the west of it, with the Pantier house still standing, while the Pantiers and everyone who loved the church were gone. At last it was torn down and now nothing is left but two concrete steps by which people entered the church, and a part of the walk that led to the steps.

Sic transit gloria mundi!

II

During Mr. Lincoln's Springfield years some of his closest minis-terial friendships were made. Such a one was the Rev. Josephus Hewett who organized the First Christian Church (Disciples) in that city. He was an evangelist of that communion known popularly in those days by the nickname "Campbellites," due to the fact that one of the founders of the movement was Alexander Campbell of Beth-any, West Virginia. That the Rev. Mr. Hewett was a warm friend of Lincoln is evidenced by the letter Mr. Lincoln wrote from Con-gress in 1848. Lincoln addressed him as "Dear Hewett," and among other things said: "For old acquaintance's sake, if for nothing else, be sure to write me on receiving this. I was very near forgetting to tell you that on my being introduced to General Quitman and tell-ing I was from Springfield, Illinois, he at once remarked, 'Then you know my valued friend, Hewett of Natchez,' and being assured that I did, he said just such things about you as I like to hear said about my own valued friends."

Hewett was born in New York City, August 27, 1805, and removed to Versailles, Kentucky, when twelve years old. He came to Illinois in 1832, settling near Jacksonville; other members of his family followed in 1838. Immediately after his arrival he began to preach, and was heard in Jacksonville, Carrollton, and elsewhere. A few followers of Alexander Campbell had drifted into Springfield from Kentucky, and Hewett was persuaded to come to Springfield and start a church of that communion in 1832. Hewett continued in charge of the Springfield church until he left for Mississippi in 1838.

James H. Matheny wrote in the Illinois State Journal, April 28, 1889: "Josephus Hewett was one of the most eloquent men I ever knew. He came here as a minister of the Christian Church. Afterward he was admitted to the Bar and appointed prosecuting attorney for the district. He was a conscientious man and had a high sense of the responsibility of his office. On the first day of each term of court it was his duty to charge the grand jury, and people invariably laid aside their work and flocked to the courthouse to hear him." Matheny further says, "his duties interfered with his obligations and friendships, and on the eve of a momentous criminal trial he resigned his office. The next morning it was announced that he had resigned his office and gone south." Justice Davis of the United States Supreme Court left this encomium: "Hewett, eloquent and persuasive, and my valued friend."

Contemporaneous with the renowned Peter Cartwright, and a crony of that picturesque exhorter and revivalist, was the Rev. Peter Akers. Abraham Lincoln is reported to have said of Akers after hearing him preach in 1837, when Lincoln was twenty-eight years of age, "It was the most instructive sermon, and he the most impressive preacher I have ever heard. It is wonderful that God has given such power to men. I firmly believe his interpretation of prophecy, so far as I understand it, and especially about the breaking down of civil and religious tyrannies; and odd as it may seem, I was deeply impressed that I should be somehow strangely mixed up with them."

Colonel James F. Jaquess of the Seventy-third Illinois Infantry Volunteers was a prominent minister of the Methodist Episcopal Church, and pastor of the First Methodist Church in Springfield for a number of years. The Colonel is described as a pulpit Boanerges, a "Son of Thunder," and he made fully as good a soldier of the Union as he was of the Cross. It was Colonel Jaquess who conceived and carried out a peace mission to Jefferson Davis, in conjunction with James R. Gilmore, writer and publicist. Nothing tangible came of the interview with President Davis, although the meeting of the men was characterized by candor and courtesy on both sides. The Rev. Ervin Chapman, D.D., in his book *New Light on Abraham Lincoln,* says: "To the reelection of Abraham Lincoln as President and the final overthrow of the Rebellion, the Jaquess-Gilmore Embassy of 1863-64 contributed more largely than did any other single effort of individuals, or any one achievement or act of the government during that period"—a pretty large order.

According to Dr. Clarence P. McClelland of MacMurray College, Jacksonville, Illinois, there is incontrovertible evidence that Abraham Lincoln was profoundly affected by the preaching of Colonel Jaquess. To prove this he cites the address delivered by Colonel Jaquess at the eleventh annual reunion of the survivors of his regiment. The preacher-soldier said:

> The mention of Mr. Lincoln's name recalls to my mind an occurrence that perhaps I ought to mention . . . I happen to know something on that subject [that is, Mr. Lincoln's religious sentiments] that very few persons know. My wife, who has been dead nearly two years, was the only witness of what I am going to state to you as having occurred . . . I was standing at the parsonage door one Sunday morning, a beautiful morning in May, when a little boy came up to me and said: "Mr. Lincoln sent me around to see if you was going to preach today." Now, I had met Mr. Lincoln, but I never thought any more of Abe Lincoln than I did of anyone else. I said to the boy: "You go back and tell Mr. Lincoln that if he will come to church he will see whether I am going to preach or not." The little fellow stood working his fingers and finally said: "Mr. Lincoln told me he would give me a quarter if I would find out whether you are going to preach." I did not

want to rob the little fellow of his income, so I told him to tell Mr. Lincoln that I was going to try to preach . . .

The church was filled that morning. It was a good-sized church, but on that day all the seats were filled. I had chosen for my text the words: "Ye must be born again," and during the course of my sermon I paid particular stress on the word "must." Mr. Lincoln came into the church after the service had commenced, and there being no vacant seats, chairs were put in the altar in front of the pulpit, and Mr. Lincoln and Governor French and wife sat in the altar during the entire service, Mr. Lincoln on my left hand and Governor French on my right, and I noticed that Mr. Lincoln appeared to be deeply interested in the sermon. A few days after that Sunday Mr. Lincoln called on me and informed me that he had been greatly impressed with my remarks on Sunday and that he had come to talk with me further on the matter. I invited him in, and my wife and I talked and prayed with him for hours. Now, I have seen persons converted; I have seen hundreds brought to Christ, and if ever a person was converted, Abraham Lincoln was converted that night in my house. His wife was a Presbyterian, but from remarks he made to me he could not accept Calvinism. He never joined my church, but I will always believe that since that night, Abraham Lincoln lived and died a Christian gentleman.

James R. Gilmore in *Down in Tennessee* says of Colonel Jaquess: "As to his life, he takes the right view about it. He considers it already given to the country . . . He is a hero, John Brown and Chevalier Bayard rolled into one, and polished up with common sense and a knowledge of Greek, Latin and the mathematics." Sandburg thinks "a fanastic tint ran through" Colonel Jaquess' proposal of the peace mission, but of the minister's sincerity and courage there is abundant evidence.

Nor should the gentle, lovable Albert Hale be forgotten, a minister whom all Springfield loved, and Abraham Lincoln knew and admired. Paul M. Angle in his book *Here I Have Lived*—the Springfield of Lincoln's residence—pays tribute to the Rev. Mr. Hale as one who "went about doing good." Does not the inscription on a memorial tablet in Westminster Presbyterian Church (formerly the Second Presbyterian Church) speak eloquently of this shepherd of souls?

To The Glory of God And
In Loving Memory of
Reverend Albert Hale
November 29, 1799——January 30, 1891
For Twenty-seven Years 1839—1866
Father Hale was Pastor of this church and
Ever Bishop of the Highways and Hedges
A friend of the poor and sorrowing and
A preacher of the Lord Jesus Christ
He was loyal to the Union
A friend and counselor to the Martyr President

III

Dr. Francis A. McNeil was both physician and preacher, not an unusual combination in the earlier days of the republic. He practiced in Springfield in the late 'thirties and in the 'forties. On May 29, 1846, Lincoln wrote to John J. Hardin: "Dr. F. A. McNeil is desirous of going into the campaign to Mexico as a surgeon, and he thinks that you, more probably than anyone else, may have the power to give him the place. If it shall turn out that you hold the power, and can consistently with the claims of others, give him the appointment, it would very much gratify many of us here, and dissatisfy none. We regard him as a very sensible and very clever man; and an excellent physician and surgeon." McNeil and Lincoln were chosen by the Masonic Lodge of Springfield to deliver the eulogy over the grave of Bowling Green, the New Salem justice of the peace in 1842.

The Rev. John G. Bergen was the founder of the First Presbyterian Church in Springfield, resided there practically all the period of Lincoln's residence. The Rev. Francis Springer, founder of the Lutheran Church in the same city, lived just across the street south of the

Lincolns. There is a story which persists that Lincoln gave him twenty-five dollars to help start his church.

The Rev. Charles Dresser, Episcopal clergyman, comes twice into the Lincoln story, once by reason of his performing the marriage ceremony for Abraham Lincoln and Mary Todd on November 4, 1842, and again by Mr. Lincoln's purchase from him in 1844 of the house he built in 1839, located on the corner of Jackson and Eighth streets. The Rev. Dr. Dresser was a New Englander by birth, and was educated at Brown University, where he was a classmate of George D. Prentice, author and editor. He settled in Springfield, Illinois in 1838, where he became the first rector of the parish now known as St. Paul's Church. After serving as professor of English in Jubilee College, Robins Nest, Peoria County, Illinois, he returned to Springfield, where after a lingering illness, he died March 25, 1865, and is buried on a hill near Lincoln's tomb.

Another preacher who figured prominently as a Springfield contemporary of Mr. Lincoln was Charles Reynolds Matheny. The part he took and the good he did far outweigh the notice he has received from historical writers. Born in Virginia, he migrated to Kentucky with his parents when he was three years old. Matheny was induced to settle in Springfield by the offer of all the county offices except that of sheriff. In 1821 the Methodist Society of Springfield held meetings in Matheny's home, but it was not until after the Presbyterians had erected that the Methodists put up a frame building at the corner of Fifth and Monroe streets. Despite his political and civic activities, Matheny was to the end of his days a zealous leader in the Methodist church, vitally interested in temperance and educational advancement, preaching and exhorting as opportunity presented.

There is abundant evidence that Charles Matheny and Abraham Lincoln were warm friends. Besides serving together on the board of trustees of Springfield, in 1839, the law firm of Stuart & Lincoln defended Mr. Matheny in a court case in 1838, and Mr. Lincoln supported Matheny's candidacy for county clerk in 1837 and 1839.

In his official capacity Matheny certified thrice to Lincoln's election to the legislature.

Major John T. Stuart wrote of Charles Matheny, "He was a good and useful man, had a pleasant, smiling countenance beaming with benevolence as if the light of Heaven were shining on him, singling him out from others." He was the father of eleven children.

Then there was the irrepressible Rev. Charles Chiniquy, a one-time Catholic priest who turned Protestant and had a large following in Illinois. He had been a client of Lincoln's, and William E. Barton says that Mr. Lincoln trusted and believed in Chiniquy. The ex-priest visited Mr. Lincoln in the White House in August 1861, June 1862 and in June 1864. Chiniquy warned the President that there were plots being formed against his life, and urged Lincoln to take every precaution.

The most interesting account of "Father" Chiniquy I have seen appears in a letter dated July 23, 1912, addressed to Willard E. King of Detroit, and signed by W. Mitchell. Some extracts follow:

I knew Father Chiniquy well when I was teaching in the Presbyterian College, Montreal. He was for years in his early manhood the priest of St. Anne's, Quebec. He was an eloquent and popular priest. He was a great worker in the Temperance Movement while still a priest in the Catholic Church. When he occasionally came to Montreal to preach he filled Notre Dame Cathedral. I went there often.

I don't know the exact circumstances which led him to quit the Roman Catholic Church. His enemies said it was because he was not made a Bishop. Anyway, he was a very able man. After his conversion to Protestantism he labored in Kankakee, Illinois, in connection with the American Presbyterian Church. He was then received into the Canadian Presbyterian Church, and preached to the end of his life in Montreal. A tabernacle was built for him in Montreal. Some of the young French Roman Catholic Priests were students in the Presbyterian College when I taught there. I think he was perfectly sincere for he endured bitter persecution while laboring in Montreal. He was fearless and frequently mobbed and sometimes thrown into prison, many times stoned while he was in Montreal. He was an eloquent and mighty man in his own language and became a great speaker in English. I think in many things he went to great extremes . . . He traveled extensively in many parts of the world. He was a great favorite with the Orangemen . . . He lectured many times in different parts of the world under their auspices.

Did Abraham Lincoln know the Rev. Dr. Edward Beecher, second son and third child of the Rev. Dr. Lyman Beecher? No record of their meeting has turned up, yet it is far more likely that they were acquainted than to assume otherwise. Rev. Edward Beecher took charge of Illinois College at Jacksonville in 1832, and during the next three years he worked hard to get a charter from the Illinois legislature. One member of that body at that time was Abraham Lincoln. If Beecher and Lincoln met, as they probably did at this particular session of the legislature, the New Englander was likely the first college-bred minister the tall member from New Salem had been privileged to meet. Assuming that they did become acquainted they surely blended chuckles as they recalled the boast of a legislator who, in opposing the charter for Beecher's college exclaimed: "I was born in a briar patch, rocked in a hog trough, and have never had my genius cramped by the pestilential air of a college."

There were still other clergymen who moved in and out upon the Illinois stage with Abraham Lincoln. Their names are included in Appendix I at the back of this book.

IV

The Springfield years touched the depths of Abraham Lincoln's brooding nature. Nothing so educates men and women as marriage and the rearing of a family. The school of the home is exacting and of long duration. Lincoln learned patience in this family course of commingled joy and sorrow. His naturally affectionate disposition deepened and greatened in the capacity of husband and father. Both Mary Todd and Abraham Lincoln were put to the acid test by their marriage, the wife gently reared and highly schooled for her day, the husband brought up in poverty and inured to privations. That they loved each other devotedly is as true as the fact that each at times tried the other sorely. But the same could be said of other married couples who, despite disparities and occasional conflicts, lived out by far the greater part of their wedded years happily and contentedly. Mary Todd Lincoln is the most tragic and libeled woman in American public life, and is deserving of sympathy and understanding rather than dispraise and caustic criticism.[1]

In Springfield, Eddie, their second-born, sickened and died, and again the mystery of existence haunted the mind and dogged the brooding nature of Lincoln. He spent long hours with Pastor James Smith in serious discussions of the Christian doctrines as they bore upon life, death and immortality. In the silence of sleepless nights Lincoln must have repeated to himself the somber lines of "Oh why should the spirit of mortal be proud?" and found no answer save a questioning faith. Nominated for the Presidency and victorious by a close vote, the President-elect left Springfield for Washington with a sad heart and a resolute purpose. Before the train left the station, in a voice choked with emotion, he spoke to a thousand of his friends and neighbors words which they were to treasure for all time. And nothing he said in the brief address was more impressive than this touching sentiment: "To His care commending you, as I hope you in your prayers will commend me, I bid you an affectionate farewell."

---

[1] A biographer says that Lincoln was "nagged into immortality," which if true, and I doubt it, isn't as bad as being lulled into mediocrity.

Chapter III

Two Gentlemen of the Cloth

"They were to the manner born."

✳✳✳✳✳✳✳✳✳✳✳✳✳✳✳✳✳✳✳✳✳✳✳✳✳✳✳✳✳✳✳✳✳✳✳✳✳✳

Among Abraham Lincoln's ministerial friends were two clergymen who stood out and above the others like twin peaks above the plain. They were the Rev. James Smith of Springfield, Illinois, and the Rev. Phineas D. Gurley of Washington, D. C. The primacy of these two preacher friends was due to the intimate pastoral relation which they bore the Lincoln family. Both of these men were old-school Presbyterians, and both were recipients of the honorary degree of Doctor of Divinity. The phrase "gentlemen of the cloth" aptly applies to them. Bearded and frock coated, they looked the eminent clergymen they were, city ministers in charge of important churches. Such were the two pastors to whom the Lincolns turned in days of bereavement.

I

Dr. James Smith was minister of the First Presbyterian Church, Springfield, Illinois, from 1849 to 1856. A Scotchman of impressive stature and a powerful orator, "Websterian," someone wrote of him, he had won fame as a polemic and author. Previous to coming to Springfield, Dr. Smith was in charge of the Presbyterian Church of Shelbyville, Kentucky, where he had made a reputation as an able sermonizer and temperance advocate. In reference to his battle against the bottle, it is worth recording that Dr. Smith prepared and preached a notable sermon from Habakkuk 1:15, "He taketh up all of them with the angle, he catcheth them in his net, and gathereth them in his drag: therefore he rejoiceth and is glad." He entitled this sermon "The Bottle, Its Evils and Its Remedy." He preached this sermon in Springfield, January 23, 1853, and it was printed at the request of thirty-nine men who heard it, one of the signers being Abraham Lincoln.

It was the death of Eddie, second son of the Lincolns which occurred in Springfield, February 1, 1850, that resulted in Mr. and Mrs. Lincoln taking a pew in the First Presbyterian Church of that city. Mrs. Lincoln, originally a Presbyterian, had united with the Episcopal Church of Springfield, but the rector of that church, the Rev. Charles Dresser, was out of the city when the little boy died, so Dr. Smith was asked to conduct the funeral service.

It is such tender pastoral ministrations that often endear clergymen to the families they have comforted in times of sorrow, and it was so in this instance. Mrs. Lincoln was admitted to membership in 1852, and both Mr. and Mrs. Lincoln attended services in the church up to the time of their leaving Springfield for Washington, February 11, 1861.

There was another circumstance which brought Mr. Lincoln and Dr. Smith into further intimacy and deepened the friendship. Following the death of Eddie, the Lincolns visited Mrs. Lincoln's relatives in Lexington, Kentucky. Some time during their stay in Mrs. Lincoln's old home town, Mr. Lincoln picked up a book written by Dr. Smith entitled *The Christian Defense* and published by J. A. James, Cincinnati, Ohio. The theological works of that period were mostly heavy reading, dogmatic and controversial, but this one was different, and Mr. Lincoln found it interesting. Not being able to finish reading the book in Kentucky, on his return to Springfield Lincoln procured a copy of *The Christian Defense*, read it through, and later discussed the work with the author. Since this book and Mr. Lincoln's interest in it bulks large in controversies about his religious views, it may be profitable to hear what Dr. Smith had to say when the endless debate on Lincoln and religion began to take shape and consume a lot of printer's ink. In a letter written from Cairns, Scotland, and dated January 24, 1867, addressed to the redoubtable William H. Herndon of Springfield, Dr. Smith wrote: [1]

> It was my honor to place before Mr. Lincoln arguments designed to prove the divine authority and inspiration of the Scriptures, accompanied by the arguments of infidel objectors, in their own language. To the arguments on both sides Mr. Lincoln gave a most patient, impartial and searching investigation. To use his own language, he examined the arguments as a lawyer who is anxious to investigate truth investigates testimony. The result was the announcement made by himself that the argument in favor of the divine authority and inspiration of the Scriptures was unanswerable.

This statement from one who was there and ought to know, cannot be successfully pooh-poohed out of court, nor does it stand alone; one has but to read Dr. William E. Barton's *The Soul of Abraham Lincoln*, Chapters XIII and Appendix VII, to find the accumulated evidence of the influence of Dr. Smith's book on Mr. Lincoln's thinking. This observation from Ninian W. Edwards, brother-in-law of Mr. Lincoln, dated December 22, 1872, is to the point: "A short time after the Rev. Dr. Smith became pastor of the First Presbyterian Church in this city, Mr. Lincoln said to me: 'I have been reading a work of Dr. Smith on the evidences of Christianity, and have

---

[1] William H. Herndon, law partner of Lincoln and author of the much controverted biography, didn't like Dr. James Smith. Dr. Barton says "Herndon's letter to Dr. Smith was impudent, demanding that he answer as a man, if he could, and if not as a man, then as a Christian—a challenge which the old Scotchman answered in kind." Those interested in this exchange of epistles between lawyer Herndon and Preacher Smith should consult the Editor's Preface in the one-volume *Herndon's Life of Lincoln* (New York: Albert & Charles Boni, 1930), "with an introduction and notes" by the distinguished Lincoln authority, Dr. Paul M. Angle.

heard him preach and converse on the subject, and am now convinced of the truth of the Christian religion.' "

Something further about *The Christian Defense* may be in order here. It is a scarce item, and it is doubtful if there are as many as twenty-five copies in existence. Dr. Barton lists ten copies, and the libraries where they are available. I know of two additional copies, my own, and a copy in the library of Thomas Irving Starr, Detroit. How I came to own a copy of *The Christian Defense* may be of interest to Lincoln students. In the early 1930's I was visiting in the office of the late Logan Hay of Springfield, a nephew of John Hay, when Mr. Hay put a copy of Dr. Smith's book into my hands and remarked: "I bought this book for twenty dollars from H. E. Barker, now of California, who used to be proprietor of a bookstore in Springfield. You should have a copy. It is hard to find, and will become increasingly so. You may have it for what it cost me, and it's a good buy at that figure."

It was a good buy, and I prize the book highly. Looking through it I have tried to account for Mr. Lincoln's interest in this theological work, and I think I have succeeded to some extent. While outmoded by the research, excavations, and scholarship of a century since its publication, for its day *The Christian Defense* was something unique in that it was a two-way discussion of the evidences of Christianity. Most similar works of Lincoln's day were one-way discussions, often dogmatic in the extreme, and handicapped by a disposition "to take the Kingdom by violence." In this book the militant unbeliever has his say as well as the devout believer. In this connection I wish to say that I do not think the statement of Dr. Smith in his letter to Mr. Herndon, important though it is, and enlightening too, proves Mr. Lincoln an orthodox Christian according to the standard of the churches of his day. I do think it reveals Lincoln's interest and high evaluation of Dr. Smith's books. I cannot but believe too, that Mr. Lincoln's words to his long time friend Joshua Speed, made but a few months before the assassination, were in some way related to and inspired by Dr. Smith's book. The Lincoln words I refer to are these: "Speed, take all of this Book [the Bible] on reason that you can, and the balance on faith, and you will live and die a better man."

Inasmuch as Mr. Lincoln never united with the church, and we have his reasons for not doing so, and knowing something of the working of his mind, it would seem that there were still "obstinate questionings" not fully answered, and obscure corners into which light had not fully come. But of the impression *The Christian Defense* made upon him, together with the conversations with its author, there can be no doubt.

The affection in which Mr. Lincoln held Dr. Smith and his confidence in the valiant Scotchman was attested by the President when he appointed him consul to Dundee, Scotland, and this despite the fact that Smith was a Democrat and a Southerner, though not a secessionist. Still another bit of evidence of the esteem in which the Lincoln family held Dr. Smith is the fact that following the President's death, his gold-headed cane was presented by the family to Dr. Smith, who in turn willed it to John Bright, the famous orator, member of the British House of Commons, and strong supporter of the United States during the Civil War.

Thus the picture that last comes before us of this gallant gentleman of the cloth—possibly a little oracular—is a big-bodied minister in long black-skirted coat, high hat, and, in his latter days, carrying the cane left him by the family of his friend and former parishioner, Abraham Lincoln. He died in the land of his birth after a lingering illness, July 3, 1871, and is buried in Glasgow.

II

The New York Avenue Presbyterian Church, Washington, D. C., is one of the shrines that followers of the Lincoln trail seek out when in the nation's capital. The brick edifice stands on New York Avenue and Thirteenth Street N. W., and the pew occupied by the Lincolns is the sixth from the front and to the left of the pulpit. Here is where Abraham Lincoln so often worshiped through the four grinding, tragic years of his Presidency; and his pastor was the Rev. Phineas D. Gurley, D.D., eminent in his chosen calling, and forever woven into the fabric of the tapestry of Lincoln lore. Of English descent, highly educated, he was dignified and proper in dress and manner, yet withal a humble and faithful servant of the Lord.

His first pastorate was the First Presbyterian Church of Indianapolis, Indiana, and not far away was the Second Presbyterian Church of which Henry Ward Beecher was the famed minister, destined to become a world figure. In 1850, Dr. Gurley became minister of the First Presbyterian Church, Dayton, Ohio, and in 1854, was installed pastor of the F Street Presbyterian Church, Washington, D. C. On the 30th of July, 1859, a union of the Second Presbyterian Church with the F Street Church was consummated, the united body being known by the present name of the New York Avenue Church. It was as minister of this church that Dr. Gurley became a national character, not only because the Lincolns became pewholders in his church, but also due to the intimate friendship with the President and Mrs. Lincoln which greatened with the war years in Washington.[2]

February 1862 was a sad birthday month for the President and Mrs. Lincoln, for on Thursday the 20th, William Wallace Lincoln, affectionately known as "Willie" died, and for the second time the biblical refrain became a threnody in the Lincoln household:

> A voice was heard in Ramah,
> Weeping and great mourning,
> Rachel weeping for her children;
> And she would not be comforted,
> because they are not.

[2] A check signed by Mr. Lincoln bearing date of January 25, 1863, drawn on the Bank of Riggs and Company, reads: "Pay to Rev. Dr. Gurley (for church) or bearer, Twenty-Five Dollars."

Willie was a bright lovely boy. Mrs. Lincoln was prostrated with grief, and scarcely less so was the President. To add to the anxiety and sorrow of the Lincolns, Tad, the younger son, was also critically ill. Dr. Gurley came to comfort and console the family. On Monday the 24th, at 2:00 P.M., the funeral took place in the East Room of the White House. Dr. Gurley, conducting the simple service with appropriate scripture readings, spoke words of consolation, and offered a prayer full of faith and comfort. No other office of a shepherd of souls is so likely to bind the hearts of a stricken household to a minister with strong cords of love than his presence there when death smites the four corners of the home.

Quite naturally it came about that Dr. Gurley was often a guest of the President and became his counselor and confidant. The record here is clear and shining. To the credit of the pastor of the New York Avenue Church, he never exploited this friendship, and to quote Dr. William E. Barton,

> Dr. Gurley's testimonies to the religious development of Lincoln's life were conservative, and bear upon their face marks of trustworthiness. There are no extravagant claims, no florid and declamatory theological affirmations, but such as this, which Dr. Gurley remembered to have heard Lincoln say to a company of clergymen calling on him in one of the darkest times in the Civil War:
> "My hope of success in this struggle rests on that immutable foundation, the justice and goodness of God; and when events are very threatening I still hope that in some way all will be well in the end because God is just, and God will be on our side."

It will be recalled that Mr. Lincoln varied this form of speech and on other occasions said he was less anxious to proclaim that God was on his side than he was to be sure that he was on God's side. In both expressions the idea is the same. The heavily-burdened President was reaching out in the darkness to find the will of God.

Dr. Gurley left an unpublished and uncompleted manuscript

which was made available to writers and others interested, by his daughter, Mrs. Eunice K. Adams, of Washington, D. C. One of the entries in the Gurley manuscript follows:

One morning, as Mr. Lincoln's pastor and intimate friend, I went over to the White House in response to an invitation from the President. He had me come over before he had his breakfast. The night before we had been together, and Mr. Lincoln had said, "Doctor, you rise early, so do I. Come over tomorrow morning about seven o'clock. We can talk for an hour before breakfast." This I did, as before stated . . . As I passed out of the gateway which leads up to the White House and stepped on the street, I was joined by a member of my congregation. "Why doctor," said my friend, "it is not nine o'clock. What are you doing at the Executive Mansion?" To this I replied, "Mr. Lincoln and I have been having a morning chat." "On the war, I suppose?" "Far from it," said I. "We have been talking of the state of the soul after death. That is a subject of which Mr. Lincoln never tires. I have had a great many conversations with him on the subject. This morning, however, I was a listener, as Mr. Lincoln did all the talking."

Dr. Gurley also reveals this intimate touch, as tender as it is beautiful: "Mr. Lincoln was very much impressed with an address I made over the coffin of his little son Willie. The day after the funeral he wrote me a note and asked me to write it out for him so he could give copies to his friends. He often spoke to me how he liked to read it over."

There are five paragraphs in the address, two of which are reproduced here:

Sad and solemn is the occasion which brings us here today. A dark shadow of affliction has fallen upon this habitation and upon the hearts of its inmates. The news thereof has already gone forth to the extremities of the country. The nation has heard it with deep and tender emotion, the eye of the nation is moistened with tears as it turns today to the Presidential Mansion. The heart of the nation sympathizes with its chief magistrate while to the unprecedented weight of civil care which presses down on him is added the burden of this domestic sorrow, and the prayers of the nation ascend to heaven on his behalf, and on behalf of his weeping family, that God's grace may be sufficient for them, and that in this hour of sore bereavement and trial they may have the presence and succor of Him Who said: "Come unto Me all ye that labor and are heavy laden and I will give you rest." Oh, that they may be enabled to lay their heads upon this infinite bosom and find, as many other smitten ones have found, that He is their truest refuge and strength and a very present help in trouble.

The beloved youth whose death we now and here lament was a child of bright intelligence and of peculiar promise. He possessed many excellent qualities of mind and heart which greatly endeared him, not only to the family circle, but to all his youthful acquaintances and friends. His mind was active, he was inquisitive and conscientious; his disposition was amiable and affectionate, his impulses kind and generous; his words and manners were gentle and attractive. It is easy to see how a child thus endowed could, in the course of eleven years, entwine himself around the hearts of those who knew him best; nor can we wonder that the grief of his affectionate mother today is like that of Rachel weeping for her children, and refusing to be comforted because they were not.

This excerpt which is about a fourth of the address, gives a comely picture of the little boy, indicates something of the literary style of the speaker, and is of a nature to comfort those who have lost children in any time or place. Lincoln mourned the loss of Willie for many months, and it is doubtful if he ever ceased to sorrow for this bright boy, a joy of the family group.

On the trip to Fortress Monroe not long after Willie had died, the President read aloud to General Wool's aide, passages from Macbeth and Hamlet, and then repeated from memory the lament of Constance for her boy:

> And, father Cardinal, I have heard you say
> That we shall see and know our friends in heaven,
> If that be true, I shall see my boy again.

In the Robert Todd Lincoln collection of Lincoln letters and documents opened July 26, 1947, there are a number of letters from Dr. Gurley to the President. Here is one dated March 30, 1864:

His Excellency, A. Lincoln,
DEAR SIR:
   According to your suggestion to Dr. Backus and myself I enclose a slip containing what seems to be an official statement of the proceedings in the Rev. Dr. Armstrong's case. It is taken from the *New Regime*, Gen'l Butler's official organ in Norfolk. If this presents the whole case, it seems to me Dr. Armstrong ought to be released. No doubt he is in thorough sympathy with the South, as decided a rebel at heart as any member of the whole cabinet; but having taken the oath of allegiance under a promise of protection if he did so, and having so far as appears said nothing, done nothing in violation of his oath, is he not fairly entitled to the protection promised him, even though he thinks Jeff Davis the greatest patriot in the world, and the Southern Confederacy the grandest and most benign government ever established by mortals.
   Pardon me Mr. President for saying that I think this business of supplying churches with pastors which the War Department seems disposed to undertake, to be not only very difficult and troublesome, but rather injurious than beneficial to the Government.
Yours truly,
P. D. GURLEY.
P.S. I enclose with this a letter from one of Dr. Armstrong's friends which I received since Dr. Backus and myself called to see you. P.D.G.

Such a letter indicates the easy friendly relation between the President and his pastor, and it also reveals the plentiful supply of common sense possessed by Dr. Gurley.

When Black Friday came on April 14, 1865, and the President was struck down by the assassin's bullet, it was Dr. Gurley who comforted the sobbing widow and the two sons, one a mature young man, the other a little lad, also greatly beloved by his father.

Sixty clergymen attended the President's funeral services in the

East Room of the White House, but it was Dr. Gurley, the President's pastor, who paid the memorial tribute, a solemn and impressive address. "A bitter cup from the hand of a chastening Divine Father" had been given the mourning nation, he said:

> His way is in the sea and His path in the great waters; and His footsteps are not known . . . We bow, we weep, we worship . . . The cruel assassin brought mysterious affliction. We will wait for His interpretation . . . He may purify us more in the furnace of trial, but He will not consume us . . . The people had in the late President a loving confidence. No man since Washington was so deeply enshrined in the hearts of the people. He deserved it, merited it by his acts, by the whole tone of his life. He leaned on God, remembering that God is history . . . On leaving Springfield he said to old and tried friends: "Pray for me." They did pray for him; and millions of others prayed for him, nor did they pray in vain.

Dr. Gurley was a member of the funeral party that traveled seventeen hundred miles by a circuitous route, stopping at the most important cities, where multitudes looked upon all that was mortal of the man who, born in a one-room cabin with a dirt floor and lighted by a single window, had climbed through toil and struggle to his place among the stars of fame. Never was there so great a funeral procession since the Israelites carried the bones of Joseph through a generation back to the old home in Canaan. Then came the last scene: Oak Ridge Cemetery, Springfield; an oration by Bishop Matthew Simpson, and the final prayer by Lincoln's friend and pastor.

In February 1868, Dr. Gurley's health became impaired, he was granted a leave of absence for a few months. He went to Philadelphia, thence to Richmond, to Brooklyn, and afterward to Clifton Springs, and then, being aware that there was little hope, he expressed the desire to be brought back to Washington that he might die there. The end came on Wednesday, April 30, 1868, at the age of fifty-two. He is buried in Glenwood Cemetery, Washington, D. C.

Not long after Willie Lincoln's death, President and Mrs. Lincoln had presented Dr. Gurley with an ebony cane, on the gold head of which was inscribed these words:

> Rev. P. D. Gurley, D.D. from Mr.
> and Mrs. Abraham Lincoln 1862

Thus it came about that the Rev. James Smith, D.D., and the Rev. Phineas D. Gurley, D.D., were alike honored by gifts of gold-headed canes from their most noted parishioners, the Abraham Lincolns of Springfield, Illinois, and Washington, D. C. Not everybody knows how to manage a walking stick, but these two gentlemen of the cloth knew no such difficulty. They were to that manner born.

Chapter IV

Peter Cartwright: "Son of Thunder"

"And pulpit drum ecclesiastick
Was beat with fist instead of
a stick."

✳✳✳✳✳✳✳✳✳✳✳✳✳✳✳✳✳✳✳✳✳✳✳✳✳✳✳✳✳✳✳✳✳✳✳✳✳✳

IN THE firmament of pioneer revivalism in America the star of Peter Cartwright does not merely twinkle—it blazes! Uneducated in any school other than the rough wilderness way, often uncouth and violent in manner, Cartwright was intelligent, imaginative, and tremendously resourceful. Fiercely controversial and partisan to the core, there was a lighter side to him in which humor was not lacking, nor a certain urbanity which flowered in his home and among friends. For his devotion to the Christian cause, courage, and really great ability, even his enemies paid him tribute of respect and admiration. He was unique.

Cartwright's place in the growth and development of the Middle West, and Illinois in particular, is much higher and more secure than many who are uninformed are willing to concede. He was more than a circuit rider; more than an eccentric revivalist; he had in him elements of statesmanship. In the course of his ministry he attended fifty-three Annual Conferences and was elected to eleven General Conferences, from 1816 to 1856.

When the General Conference of the Methodist Episcopal Church convened in New York City in 1844, an epochal gathering, Cartwright was one of the one hundred and eighty delegates, who included such eminent men as Matthew Simpson, later to attain renown as a bishop and to win the friendship of Abraham Lincoln; Henry B. Bascom, famed as a pulpit orator of superior eloquence; William Capers and A. B. Longstreet—names to conjure with in religious and political circles. This General Conference, it will be recalled, was the sad and solemn one which resulted in the division of American Methodism over the issue of slavery.

I

Peter Cartwright was born in Virginia, the son of a Revolutionary soldier. He emigrated to Kentucky, and following his conversion, evangelized in Ohio and Indiana, settling in Central Illinois in 1824. A friend who knew him intimately thus describes the revivalist:

> He was then about forty years old with an attractive and strongly marked physique, nearly six feet in height, erect and vigorous. His large well-formed head was covered with closely curling coal-black hair, and poised on a short, thick neck. A large round clean-shaven face with small, bright, piercing eyes, small Grecian nose, and a mouth at once mobile, expressive and firm. His hands and feet were rather small, his step elastic and decided.

Abraham Lincoln and Peter Cartwright were contemporaries for many years, and resided during that time within twenty-five miles or less of each other. Lincoln was much the younger man. It may be that these rivals politically never met prior to 1832, when both were candidates for the state legislature. That year Lincoln was defeated and Cartwright elected, this being Lincoln's only defeat at the hands of the people.

In 1846 Lincoln defeated the Methodist Boanerges in a spirited campaign in which Lincoln was assailed as an "infidel" and of all things, an "aristocrat"; this latter charge made probably because he had married aristocratic Mary Todd of Kentucky. In connection with this election there occurred a mirth-rocking episode, the telling of which, like the brook, will go on forever.

During the campaign Lincoln went to a revival meeting where Cartwright was to preach. In the course of the meeting Cartwright announced: "All who desire to lead a new life, to give their hearts to God and go to heaven, will stand." Quite a few stood up. Then the preacher raised his voice and roared: "All who do not wish to go to hell will stand." All stood up except Mr. Lincoln. Cartwright was quick to note the exception, and in solemn tones he said:

"I observe that many responded to the first invitation to give their hearts to God and go to heaven, and I further observe that all of you save one indicated you did not wish to go to hell. The sole exception is Mr. Lincoln, who did not respond to either invitation. May I enquire of you, Mr. Lincoln, where you are going?"

Lincoln rose slowly, the eyes of all upon him. "I came here," he said, "as a respectful listener. I did not know I was to be singled out by Brother Cartwright; I believe in treating religious matters with due solemnity. I admit that the questions propounded by Brother Cartwright are important. I did not feel called upon to answer as the rest did. Brother Cartwright asks me directly where I am going. I desire to reply with equal directness:—'I am going to Congress!' "

Carl Sandburg, whose version of the episode this account follows, adds: "The meeting broke up," which was just about all that meeting could do; anything else would have been anticlimax.

Another arresting aspect of the Lincoln-Cartwright campaign for Congress was revealed when the poll book of District No. 2 Springfield, where Lincoln cast his ballot was examined. It showed that Cartwright polled eight votes, Lincoln sixteen, and that the latter voted for Cartwright. Unusual, you say? Perhaps it was, but then Abraham Lincoln was himself unusual, and also magnanimous.

An account of his contests with Cartwright was given by Lincoln himself in a letter which came to light only recently, written to one John Coulter, a Michigan farmer who lived near Niles, that state. The references to Cartwright are interesting and important.

Private
Springfield, Ill., Sept. 4, 1860
John Coulter, Esq.
DEAR SIR:

Yours of the 29th is received; and I presume I understand what has prompted you to write it. In 1832, I was first a candidate for the Legislature, with some 10 or a dozen other candidates. Peter Cartwright and three others were elected, of whom I was not one. In 1834 he, and I, and several others, again became candidates; he declined before the election. I saw the race through, and, with three others, was elected. In 1835 he became a candidate to fill a vacancy in the State Senate and his sole competitor, Job Fletcher, beat him by near 600 majority.

In 1836, 1838, and 1840, I was successively elected to the Legislature, he not being a candidate at either of those elections.

I then ceased to be a candidate for anything till 1846, when I ran for Congress. Mr. Cartwright was my competitor, and I beat him, as I recollect 1,511 majority, being about double the party majority of the district.

I was never a candidate for Congress at any other time, and never had any contests with Mr. Cartwright other than as I have stated.

Please do not make this public.

Yours truly,
A. LINCOLN.

With the single sheet of writing paper, enscribed on both sides, is an envelope addressed to John Coulter, Esq., in Lincoln's hand. It bears the postmark "Springfield, Ill., Sept. 5, 1860," and a three-cent stamp.

In 1856 Cartwright published his *Autobiography*, a book of more than five hundred pages, a work which could be accurately described by the threadbare phrase "a great human document." James Russell Lowell thought it an important contribution to American literature, original, and of absorbing interest. The book abounds in vivid, dramatic, and humorous incidents, written with disarming artlessness, and stamped with the seal of sincerity. Here is a paragraph in which the revivalist describes an old time camp meeting, the like of which this generation can scarcely imagine:

The meeting was protracted for weeks, and was kept up day and night. Thousands heard of the mighty work, and came on foot, on horseback and in wagons. It was supposed that there were in attendance at different times from twelve to twenty-five thousand. Hundreds fell prostrate under the mighty power of God as men slain in battle; and it was supposed that between one and two thousand souls were happily and powerfully converted to God during the meetings. It was not unusual for as many as seven preachers to be addressing the listening thousands at the same time from different stands. At times, more than a thousand persons broke out into loud shoutings all at once, and the shouts could be heard for miles around.

On one occasion as Cartwright began his sermon he was interrupted by a persistent but ineffectual attempt of a saintly old sister to "shout." A trifle exasperated, Cartwright turned to her and said: "Dear sister, never shout as a matter of duty; when you can't help it, shout, *but never as a mere matter of duty.*"

Cartwright was as handy with his fists as he was with his horse or in the mastery of a public service. When hecklers or drunken men interrupted his meeting he suspended delivery of the sermon and tossed the trouble makers out with dispatch and for good, unless they returned in penitence and humility.

At a camp meeting on the banks of the Cumberland in the early years of the last century, an attempt was made by a gang of desperadoes to break up a service which Cartwright was conducting. To this end a burly ruffian stalked to the front of the pulpit and with an oath commanded Cartwright to "dry up." At that Cartwright suspended divine service for a few minutes, threw off his coat, descended from the pulpit, sprang upon the disturber, knocked him down and pummeled him until the fellow bellowed for mercy. Cartwright withheld that boon until the contrite bully promised to repent, and had been given the humblest seat in the "Amen corner"; then, having disposed of this little business Cartwright put on his coat, returned to the pulpit, and began anew with the words, "As I was saying brethren," and went on with the sermon.

This fiery exhorter had a contempt for college-bred ministers and was prone to belittle the ministrations of city preachers, although, as he grew older he modified his criticisms of these more polished brethren to some extent. A favorite story which he loved to repeat was this: "I recollect once to have come across one of these Latin and Greek scholars, a regular graduate in theology. In order to bring me into contempt in a public company he addressed me in Greek. In my younger days I had learned considerable German. I listened to him as if I understood it all, and then replied in Dutch. This he knew nothing about; neither did he understand Hebrew. He concluded that I had answered him in Hebrew, and immediately caved in and stated to the company that I was the first educated Methodist preacher he ever saw."

Not without wile and cunning, this Illinois Boanerges was fearless and unawed by human greatness. Preaching near Nashville, Tennessee, he was informed just as he went into the pulpit that General Andrew Jackson was among his hearers, so he thundered: "And who is Andrew Jackson? If he's a sinner God'll damn him to hell . . . the same as a Guinea nigger."

This is rough pulpit language even for Cartwright's day, although the sulphuric vapors that accompanied it were common enough in that period. Still, not all the people of Cartwright's generation relished or approved of such harsh harangues in the name of the Lord, and one of these was Abraham Lincoln. If the Springfield barrister was cold to Cartwright's theology, we may be sure that he warmed up to Peter's scornful critique of a deacon who prayed a cold perfunctory prayer: "Brother, three prayers like that would freeze hell over."

One of Cartwright's intimate friends was a fellow Illinois Methodist, the Rev. Peter Akers, D.D., an able preacher, and a good deal of a wag. It was Akers who procured a degree as Doctor of Divinity for Cartwright. On learning of this honor Peter accused Akers of having done it out of sheer loneliness at being the only Methodist Doctor of Divinity in the state. These two Peters were a precious pair. In a meeting where Cartwright was present, Akers declared to his congregation, which was behind in his salary, "If you people don't pay me my salary, so I can support my family, I shall be compelled to discontinue the ministry, and do something that will afford them a comfortable support." Peter Cartwright sprang to his feet and said: "Peter Akers, I am an older man than you are, and I never talked to my people like that in my life. If I couldn't get enough wool from the sheep, I'd shear the goats."

II

Peter was not so successful in the pulpit when he preached in the city churches of the east. He had less than usual of what John Wesley called "liberty of the spirit" in such circumstances. In his *Autobiography* he acknowledged that he failed when he preached in Boston churches during the General Conference which met there in 1852. He tells us that he preached twice: once in the Church Street Church, where he took for his text Hebrews 10:22, "let us draw near with a true heart in full assurance of faith, having our hearts sprinkled from an evil conscience, and our bodies washed with pure water." And again, the same Sunday, in the Russell Street Church, where his text was Job 22:21, "Acquaint now thyself with him, and be at peace: thereby good shall come unto thee." In both instances the people who heard him were disappointed, and plainly showed it. Peter's account of what followed his sermon in the Church Street Church is told with characteristic frankness, and with more humility than was his wont, thus:

> We had a large congregation; several preachers present; and supposing that most of the congregation had hardly ever seen or heard of

me, and that they were an educated people, and had been used to great preaching, I put on all the gravity that I well could command; I tried to preach one of my best sermons in a plain, grave, sober manner; and although I never thought myself a great preacher, yet I really thought I had done very near my best that time. Well, when I came down from the pulpit, a brother preacher introduced me to several of the prominent members of the congregation, and as I was introduced to them, they asked me very emphatically, "Is this Peter Cartwright from Illinois, the old Western pioneer?"

I answered them, "Yes, I am the very man."

"Well," said several of them, "brother, we are much disappointed; you have fallen very much under our expectations; we expected to hear a much greater sermon than you preached today."

"Well, brethren," said I, "how can it be helped? I did as well as I could, and was nearly at the top of my speed."

Peter was not so humble when he asked a Dr. Cummings, who had charge of placing the delegates in pulpits, not to give him another appointment in Boston during the General Conference, "for" said Cartwright, "your people here have not got sense enough to know a good sermon when they hear it." Nor did he stop with this tart remark. He told another Boston critic: "I could give people ideas, but I could not give them the capacity to receive these ideas."

The trouble was that Peter was not in his element amidst formal services, paid quartets, and, as Peter put it: "your old wooden organ bellowing up in the gallery." His sermons simply didn't "click" in such surroundings.

On this same eastern trip Cartwright preached for the celebrated "Father" Taylor at Bethel Charge, and had a great time of it. He took for his text Matthew 11:12, "And from the days of John the Baptist until now the kingdom of heaven suffereth violence, and the violent take it by force." Peter took it just so, that day, and his hearers were not only overjoyed, many souls were saved! Speaking in that mission for sailors, Cartwright was at home and lived fully up to the reputation which had preceded him.

·III

One golden evening as I sat in the home of Adlai E. Stevenson at Bloomington, Illinois, the former Vice-President of the United States got on the subject of Peter Cartwright. He told story after story, and concluded with a description of the old revivalist's appearance before the Democratic State Convention, which met in Springfield in the early spring of 1860. In the midst of the proceedings a delegate called attention to the fact that the venerable Peter Cartwright was present, and said he knew the Convention would be glad to hear him. Immediately there were cries of "Cartwright!" "Cartwright!" "We want to hear Cartwright!" From his seat, surrounded by the Sangamon County delegates, the venerable and famed revivalist arose and with deep emotion began:

"My friends, and fellow citizens, I am happy to be with you on the present occasion. My sun is low down on the horizon, and the days of my pilgrimage are nearly numbered. I have lived in Illinois during the entire period of its history as a state. I have watched with tender interest its marvelous growth from its feeble condition as a Territory, until it has reached its present splendor as a state. I have traveled over its prairies, slept with only the canopy of heaven for a covering; I have followed the trail of the Indians, fought the desperadoes, swam the rivers, threaded the almost pathless forests, in order that I might carry the tidings of the blessed gospel to the loneliest cabin upon the border. Yes, my friends, for seventy long years, amid appalling difficulties and dangers, I have waged an incessant warfare against the world, the flesh, the devil, and *all the other enemies of the Democratic party*." Then he took his seat amid an ovation. Incidentally, a study of this fragment of speech reveals the speaker's power before an audience. Cartwright was a natural orator of magnetic power.

Curiously, Cartwright failed to mention in his *Autobiography* the name of Abraham Lincoln. Why this omission? Possibly because the book was published in 1857, and Lincoln had not yet become a national figure; he became such following the debates with Douglas in 1858. Or, the omission may have been deliberate; the two men did not have much in common, and they were political rivals. Happily there is in the records something to compensate for the failure of Cartwright to mention his great rival's name in the *Autobiography*.

According to Henry B. Rankin, in his *Personal Recollections of Abraham Lincoln*, Cartwright changed his politics before he died, and came to the defense of President Lincoln. It was in 1862, and the Methodist minister was guest at a dinner party in New York. To his surprise and dismay he found himself in a nest of caustic critics of Mr. Lincoln. He stood it as long as he could, then replied in sturdy rebuttal: "As the crow flies," he said, "I have lived within a score of miles of Abraham Lincoln for a third of a century. Until shortly before he took the oath of office as President of the United States, we had trained in different political camps, he a Whig and I a Democrat. I remained a Democrat until the firing on Fort Sumter. Since then I know no party save that of my undivided country, and Abraham Lincoln its President." [1]

In 1874 the Lincoln Tomb in Oakridge Cemetery, Springfield, was completed at a cost of two hundred thousand dollars. When it was in process of construction Peter Cartwright dedicated a Methodist church in Menard County. At the close of the sermon he made a characteristic appeal for money with which to finish the church, and said: "The people of the country are excited over the erection of a monument to Abe Lincoln at Springfield, and are contributing liberally of their means for its completion. This is all very well, but, my friends, I am engaged in building a monument to the Lord

[1] According to Mr. Rankin, Peter Cartwright related this incident to him in 1862, and said that it took place at a dinner party that year given him by James Harper, the publisher.

Jesus Christ. This monument is the house in which we are assembled, and I want you to contribute enough to complete it." [2]

Cartwright died September 25, 1872, and is buried in the quiet little cemetery at Pleasant Plains, in the section of Illinois he so greatly loved and where he had lived since 1824. The stone at his grave bears the words of the hymn by Charles Wesley:

> Servant of God well done!
> Thy glorious warfare past;
> The battle's fought, the race is won,
> And thou art crowned at last.

[2] In the last chapter of Cartwright's *Autobiography* he gives a statistical account of his stewardship as a servant of the Lord and a Methodist preacher. Epitomized it totals 14,600 sermons; received into the Methodist church on probation and letters 10,000; baptized 8,000 children, 4,000 adults; preached at 500 funerals; contributed to the church and its organizations $2,300. These are the high points. These and other items fill two pages.

Chapter V

Bishop Matthew Simpson

The Patrick Henry of American Methodism.

****

"God bless the Methodist churches." So spoke Abraham Lincoln to a delegation of Methodist ministers who came to the White House in May 1864, to assure him their churches, north and west, were solidly behind him in his struggle to preserve the Federal Union. First and last Mr. Lincoln's acquaintance with the Methodist clergy was extensive and close. Besides Peter Cartwright and Peter Akers, pioneer preachers of Methodism, he had known and respected in the Springfield years Charles Reynolds Matheny, Jacob M. Early, and James F. Jacquess, proclaimers all of the gospel in the traditions of John Wesley. In the Washington years two eminent Methodist leaders had ready access to the White House, namely, Bishop Edward Ames and Bishop Matthew Simpson, the Patrick Henry of American Methodism, and, next to Lincoln's pastor Dr. Gurley, the most intimate of Lincoln's ministerial friends during the war years.

I

Bishop Simpson was born in Cadiz, Ohio, June 21, 1811. He came of sturdy English and Scotch ancestry, and was in his own way a learned man, "self-educated by absorption," as one writer puts it. He read the German Bible without a dictionary, and acquired a

working knowledge of Latin, Greek, and Hebrew. He was an omnivorous reader, and began to preach as a circuit rider while still in
his early twenties. He was the minister of Liberty Street Church,
Pittsburgh, for a brief period, taught in a small Methodist College
in western Pennsylvania, and then became president of Asbury
University at Greencastle, Indiana, now De Pauw, and served as
editor of *The Christian Advocate*. But it was his marvelous gift of
preaching and platform eloquence that gave him a reputation second
only to that of Henry Ward Beecher.

Simpson was like Beecher in power of stirring oratory, but here
the resemblance ends. Beecher was not above the average height and
inclined to stoutness; Simpson was tall and spare; Beecher exuded
radiant health, scarcely knowing a day of sickness; Simpson battled
with ill health, and his life was despaired of at several periods in his
busy career. In 1852, Matthew Simpson was elected a Bishop of the
Methodist Episcopal Church at the General Conference in Boston.
For the next thirty-two years his fame as preacher greatened, not
only throughout America, but in England, Scotland, Ireland, and
many other European nations. With the advent of the Civil War
the Bishop cast his wide influence and eloquent tongue on the
side of the Union and against the hateful institution of slavery. In
pulpit and on platform he moved vast crowds with the grand sweep
of his powerful speech, and the ardor of his patriotism fired the
hearts of multitudes.

The phrase "the Patrick Henry of American Methodism" as applied to Bishop Simpson is one that I am confident I can justify.
The record is clear on this point . . . contemporary evidence there
is in abundance. As for his published sermons and addresses, while
they reveal an orderly mind, a nice rhetorical balance, good argument,
and a vivid intensity, they do not, as in the printed pages of Beecher
or Webster, give the power of Simpson's personality. Henry Clay's
published speeches suffer in the same way.

The Rev. Dr. O. S. Munsell, who was a student at Asbury University in 1842, describes a sermon he heard Matthew Simpson preach from the text in Joel 3:14, "Multitudes, multitudes, in the valley of decision: for the day of the Lord is near in the valley of decision." "In the outset," says Dr. Munsell, "he pointed out what he understood to be the literal meaning of and application of the text; but said that, in a proper sense and without violence to the spirit of the divine message, it might be applied directly to the great multitude gathered that day; and that he could truthfully address them personally and say as a messenger of God, 'Multitudes, multitudes, in the valley of decision.' He then proceeded to consider the people before him in groups in the light of their personal characters as God saw them: the scorner, the hardened sinner, the hypocrite, the backslider, the penitent, and the child of God; and he portrayed each type of character with such clearness, vividness and power, that its personality seemed to stand before us a living thing."

Dr. Munsell continues with a portrayal of the increasing spell of the preacher's oratory over his audience as he reached a great climax, describing the glorified Christ "leading the hosts of God's elect children from the judgment bar to the gates of heaven while the angels cried 'lift up your heads, O ye gates, and be ye lifted up ye everlasting doors, and the King of Glory shall come in.'

"At this point the preacher seemed wholly to lose all consciousness of the presence of the vast, excited multitude, hanging upon his words, and, with lifted eyes he soared upward and still upward, till human souls could endure no more; and as with a voice of many waters, the multitude of the people in the great altar sprang to their feet, with shouts and cries, and tears and laughter."

In other instances and particularly so in the Bishop's patriotic addresses, men beat the floor with their canes or umbrellas, women tossed their fans in the air, and almost witout exception both on religious and patriotic occasions, as the Bishop completed his sermon or address, the audiences got to their feet, cheering and applauding wildly. Even when concession is made that Simpson was preaching to an emotional people in an emotional age, and that a great and terrible war was in process, the fact remains that this Patrick Henry of American Methodism was capable of overwhelming speech and deserves to rank with the great Virginia orator.

II

It is likely that Abraham Lincoln had met and heard Matthew Simpson before the terrible war broke devastatingly over the nation. The Bishop's biographer, Dr. Crooks, says: "I am informed that conferences between them [Lincoln and Simpson] took place in Springfield, Mr. Lincoln's home, during the Winter of 1860-61. While the war lasted the Bishop was often invited to come to Washington for consultation with the President and Mr. Stanton . . . Bishop Simpson's advent in the war office was usually followed by an invitation to the Secretary's private room, where long conferences were held, ending sometimes at Mr. Stanton's request, in earnest prayer."

The Rev. Dr. Thomas Bowman, who later became a bishop in the Methodist Episcopal Church, was chaplain of the United States Senate during the latter part of the war. He supplied Bishop Simpson's biographer with these observations:

In 1864-65, as I spent several months in Washington, I often heard members of Congress and other distinguished visitors say that they heard the President frequently express his great respect for and confidence in Bishop Simpson. It was well known that the President occasionally sent for the Bishop in order to procure information about the affairs of the nation. The President said in substance, "Bishop Simpson is a wise and thoughtful man. He travels extensively over the country and sees things as they are. He has no axe to grind, and therefore I can depend upon him for such information as I need."

On one occasion, with two or three friends, I was conversing with Mr. Lincoln near the distant window in the "Blue Room," when unexpectedly the door opened and Bishop Simpson entered. Immediately the President raised both arms and started for the Bishop almost on a run. When he reached him he grasped him with both hands and exclaimed: "Why, Bishop Simpson, how glad I am to see you!" In a few moments we retired and left them alone. I afterward learned that they spent several hours in private, and that this was one of the times when the Bishop had been specially invited by the President to come to Washington for such an interview.

This famed Methodist preacher-orator had a lecture on "Our Country," which he delivered many times during the war years, and always with tremendous effect. On an important occasion he gave this lecture in one of the Methodist churches in Washington, and President Lincoln was in the audience, enjoying every word and joining in the applause, when the Bishop, who had been discoursing on America as a land of opportunity, paused and said: "Why, it is commonly reported that a rail splitter has been elected President of the United States."

At the close of the lecture Mr. Lincoln strode down the aisle, and taking the Bishop warmly by the hand, exclaimed in a voice so loud that it could be heard all around: "Bishop Simpson, that was a splendid lecture." Then in a lower tone and with a broad smile lighting his face, Lincoln said: "But you didn't strike the ile." The Bishop caught the point and replied, "Mr. President, I am surprised at myself to see that while I have thought so much about the great resources of the country, I should have entirely overlooked our oil interests. I shall not do so again." Dr. Bowman, who overheard this conversation and also heard the Bishop give the same lecture on another occasion, says, "The next time I heard the lecture the Bishop struck 'the ile,'—and well he might!"

Dr. Crooks thinks that after Mr. Stanton came into the Cabinet, the Bishop's relation with the President became more intimate. He likewise says that Mr. Lincoln used Bishop Simpson to modify the War Secretary's extreme views, and to soften Stanton's disposition to treat with severity the "border rebels" who stayed at home and gave aid and comfort to the enemy. Stanton and the Bishop both resided in Cadiz, which may help to account for the Secretary's liking for the clergyman, and his willingness to take advice from him.

Dr. Clarence True Wilson, in an article in *Current History* for October 1929, credited Bishop Simpson with inspiring President Lincoln to issue the Emancipation Proclamation. The Bishop's biographer does not make this claim, but he does say that as far back as 1861, Simpson had indicated to Mr. Lincoln that such action was necessary:

> He believed, from the first, that emancipation would come out of the war, and in discussing General Fremont's proclamation of 1861 which Lincoln annulled, the Bishop said had he been in Fremont's place he would have done the same. Bishop Simpson, along with other leading Republicans, was impatient with Lincoln's apparent slowness to proclaim Emancipation. The President had good reasons for delay in this important matter. When Moncure D. Conway, a noted liberal preacher of his day urged Emancipation upon the President just after the Bull Run defeat, Lincoln said to him: "Go and educate the people up to it, and I will issue the proclamation." Bishop Simpson was doing just that through those fateful years, and doing it continually.

On November 3, 1864, in the Academy of Music, New York, with the Presidential election but a few days off, Bishop Simpson made his famous war speech in which he pleaded for the election of Mr. Lincoln over General McClellan. The Bishop spoke for two hours, and concluded with this paragraph, which is evidently taken from a stenographer's report:

> Your Fifty-fifth Regiment carried this flag (taking up a war-worn, shot-riddled flag, which was greeted with cheers); it has been at New Dern, and at South Mountain, and at Antietam. The blood of our brave boys is upon it; the bullets of rebels have gone through and through it; yet it is the same old flag, (most enthusiastic applause, the audience rising and giving three rousing cheers) our fathers followed that flag; we expect that our children and our children's children will

follow it; there is nothing on earth like that old flag for beauty, (long and loud cheering) long may those stars shine! Just now there are clouds upon it, and mists gathering around it, but the stars are coming out, and others are joining them, and they grow brighter and brighter, and so may they shine till the last star in the heavens shall fall! (Great cheering and waving of handkerchiefs and hurrahing.)

An eloquent speech, yes, but one that Abraham Lincoln could ot have made. Flag waving was not for him who had said, "I have ot only suffered by the South, I have suffered *with* the South." ʼet the President leaned upon Bishop Simpson, and since somebody ʾho could speak so eloquently and with such patriotic ardor was ceeded at so critical an election, it must have comforted Abraham ₁incoln to know that the person to do it was Bishop Matthew impson.

III

Bishop Simpson's last great service to the memory of Abraham ₁incoln was his eulogy at the burial of the President on May 4th, 865, in Oak Ridge Cemetery, Springfield, Illinois. A sea of faces ʾas before him and about him. Many were present who had known ₕe President in the old days, those who had voted for him and ₉ainst him; old friends and new friends were there, the great from ₕe nation's capital, and the humble and the obscure were in that ₕuge silent throng. The Bishop was used to great throngs of people ₒme to hear him speak, but nothing in his experience compared ʾith this vast silent and expectant multitude. He had never faced ₕch massed acres of human beings before, nor would he ever so ₒ again. His voice was not uncommonly strong, and no doubt he ʾondered how many of such a multitude could hear him and follow ₕs words. It was a testing time for even the most experienced and ₕfted of speakers.

The Bishop measured up well to the ordeal, although in cold ₕrint his eulogy suffers when compared with that of Henry Ward

Beecher delivered in Brooklyn eight days previous. But if the Bishop's rhetoric is not so uniformly sustained, nor his imagery quite so mournfully magnificent as Beecher's, Simpson's tribute is more intimate, and very full of comfort to a sorrowing nation.

He began by addressing the people as "Fellow Citizens of Illinois and many parts of our entire Union." He referred to the farewell speech of Lincoln on leaving Springfield, and contrasted the President's leaving Springfield, with his homecoming. In measured sentences he strove to describe the sorrow of the people when the awful word went the country around that Lincoln had fallen. "Men of all political parties and of all religious creeds have united in paying this tribute," the Bishop said. "The Archbishop of the Catholic Church in New York and a Protestant walked side by side in the sad procession, and a Jewish rabbi performed a part of the solemn service." Next he dealt with Abraham Lincoln as a man of faith, saying:

> Abraham Lincoln was a good man; he was known as an honest, temperate, forgiving man; a just man; a man of noble heart in every way. As to his religious experience I cannot speak definitely, because I was not privileged to know much of his private sentiments . . . My acquaintance with him did not give me the opportunity to hear him speak on these topics. This I know, however, he read the Bible frequently, loved it for its great truths, and he tried to be guided by its precepts. He believed in Christ the Saviour of Sinners, and I think he was sincere in trying to bring his life in harmony with the principles of revealed religion. Certainly if there ever was a man who illustrated some of the principles of pure religion, that man was our departed President. Look over all his speeches, listen to his utterances. He never spoke unkindly of any man. Even the rebels received no word of anger from him. As a ruler, I doubt if any President has ever shown such trust in God, or in public documents so frequently referred to divine aid. Often did he remark to friends and delegations that his hope for our success rested in his conviction that God would bless our efforts because we were trying to do right. To the address of a large religious body he replied: "Thanks be unto God, who, in our trials, giveth us the churches . . ."

Then came the Bishop's apostrophe with which he ended the ılogy:

Chieftain, farewell! The nation mourns thee. Mothers shall teach thy name to their lisping children; the youth of our land shall emulate thy virtues; statesmen shall study thy record, and from it learn lessons of wisdom. Mute though thy lips be, yet they still speak. Hushed is thy voice, but its echoes of liberty are ringing through the world, and the sons of bondage listen with joy. Thou did'st fall not for thyself. The assassin had no hate for thee; our hearts were aimed at; our national life was sought. We crown thee as our martyr of Humanity, enthrone thee as her triumphant son. Hero, martyr, friend, farewell!

On June 15, 1884, the Patrick Henry of American Methodism nished his course in Philadelphia. He had fought a good fight, and ad kept the faith!

Chapter VI

Owen Lovejoy:
Fiery Abolitionist Preacher

Lincoln loved this servant of the Lord.

****

IN THE spring of 1850, a "prairie schooner," as emigrant wagon
were called in pioneer days, rattled into Princeton, Illinois. O
Sunday the husband, wife and young son went to the leading chur
of that town. In later years the boy, who had become a soldier i
the Civil War, attaining the rank of colonel, and then a memb
of Congress, recalled that Sunday morning in church in the followi
descriptive passage:

At Princeton we attended Divine Worship in the Congregation
Church, and were surprised as well as pleased to find ourselves amor
as intelligent and cultivated people as we had ever seen, most of the
emigrants from New England and New York. But when the past
ascended the pulpit, we were even more surprised. Instead of a bac
woods preacher such as we had read accounts of in the West, it w
apparent that this pastor was a man of both culture and characte
He was a little above the medium height, of sturdy but not too sto
figure, full face, broad and massive forehead surmounted by heav
brown hair, large kindly beaming eyes, a large cheery mouth and broa
strong chin. His head was well set upon broad shoulders, and his who
bearing was such as to indicate that while his was a merry and even
jovial nature, he was one of those strong characters who can do an
dare.

I do not remember the text, nor do I remember much that the preacher said, except that he talked of the fugitive slave law, and described the poor panting fugitive whose only crime was that he was black and fleeing for liberty, and denounced the law that made it the duty of the officers of the United States to pursue him, and that gave them authority to summon and require every citizen to join in the chase, "making slave-catchers of us all," declaring that there was no power on earth that could make a slave-catcher of him, and that he would never obey the law, quoting texts from the Bible to sustain him. He made the most thrilling appeal for the poor fugitive, but his denunciation of the slave-catcher was appalling. He characterized the President of the United States as the chief slave-catcher of all.

As we passed out of the church I came upon our new acquaintance, Mr. Green. Before we could say a word, he exclaimed: "They'll kill him sho' jes' the same as they killed his brother 'Lijah, that's what they'll do! I saw a man this morning thet would sooner kill him then he would a dog!"

That preacher was the Rev. Owen Lovejoy, fiery Abolitionist preacher and warm friend and stalwart supporter of Abraham Lincoln.

I

Owen Lovejoy was born at Albion, Maine, January 6, 1811. He attended Bowdoin College but did not graduate; studied law, taught school, and in 1833 went to Alton, Illinois to prepare for the ministry under the tutelage of his brother, Elijah P. Lovejoy, who had embraced the Abolition cause with the zeal of a crusader. Owen was not long in enlisting in the same crusade, and when on November 7, 1837, Elijah was brutally murdered by a mob of proslavery men, Owen knelt by the lifeless body of his brother and vowed: "never to forsake the cause that had been sprinkled with his brother's blood." That vow he kept.

After completing his theological studies, he was called to the ministry of the Congregational Church at Princeton, Illinois, where he served ably for seventeen years. Never neglecting his parish duties,

Lovejoy soon became the eloquent orator of Abolition in Illinois, often encountering opposition, and sometimes violence. He early got into politics, casting his lot with the newly organized Republican party, was elected to the Illinois legislature in 1854, and in 1856 was elected to Congress in which he served conspicuously until his death at Brooklyn, New York, in 1864. Just when and where Lovejoy first met Mr. Lincoln is not clear, but a passage in a letter from the President dated May 30, 1864, in reply to one from John H. Bryant inviting him to attend a meeting preliminary to erecting a monument to Lovejoy is illuminating. Mr. Lincoln wrote:

"Many of you have known Mr. Lovejoy longer than I have, and are better able than I to do his memory complete justice. My personal acquaintance with him commenced only about ten years ago, since when it has been quite intimate, and every step in it has been one of increasing respect and esteem ending, with his life, in no less than affection on my part. . . . He was my most generous friend."

The late Joseph G. Cannon, speaker of the House of Representatives, and a picturesque figure in American politics, was present as a young man on an occasion when Lovejoy spoke under threat of his life. The incident took place in Greenup, Cumberland County, Illinois, which was proslavery in sentiment. It was a hostile crowd Lovejoy faced that day, and he knew it. He arose, and with grave deliberation said:

"I have been told that Owen Lovejoy would not be here today, and that if he did come he would not be allowed to speak. The oldest member of my family lies in his grave over at Alton on the Mississippi, a victim of mob violence. He died in defense of liberty. It is the most a man can do in any cause. I will speak here today."

The crowd stirred uneasily, but listened closely as Lovejoy continued: "I am called an Abolitionist. Some Republicans are afraid of me. If I am an Abolitionist, make the most of it, and you must know there are many more like me." He looked over the crowd as if gauging its hostility as he said: "I'll try this case, and I want twelve men, all of them Democrats, to stand up." . . . After a pause he continued: "You will well and truly hear the statement touching the question I am about to put, and a true verdict render as you shall answer at the last judgment day." . . . A longer pause, then he resumed:

On a plantation, in the distant Southland, in the low miasmatic swamps, there was a woman. She was young, handsome, and under God's law had as much right to live and control her own actions as any of us. She was of one-eighth African blood, just like your blood and mine. The overseer of the plantation where she was held in bondage sought to persecute her because she would not assent to his advances. She escaped into the swamps. Bloodhounds were set on her trail. She boarded a little steamboat which plied on a small river which emptied into the great Father of Waters. In the fullness of time she landed at the first station in Illinois, name not given, and proceeded from station to station. Finally she arrived in Princeton. I myself was the keeper of that station at Princeton. She came to my house hungry and told me her story. She was fairer than my own daughter, proud, tall and beautiful. She was naked and I clothed her; she was hungry and I gave her bread; she was penniless and I gave her money. She was unable to reach the next station and I sent her to it. So from station to station she crossed the Northland far from baying dogs on her trail, and out from under the shadow of the flag we love and venerate, into Canada. Today she lives there a free and happy woman.

As Lovejoy reached the end of this dramatic recital it was reported that women sobbed and men swore . . . Lovejoy surveyed the crowd and thundered: "As you shall answer to God, what would you have done? Get up, rise men and give your verdict." And men rose up and shouted back: "You did right. We would have done the same."

This thrilling episode is a pretty good index to the character of the Rev. Owen Lovejoy, Abolitionist and friend of Abraham Lincoln.

II

During the turbulent war years Lincoln and Lovejoy saw much of
each other, and it is doubtful if the President had a more loyal and
zealous supporter. This is all the more remarkable because Lincoln
was not an Abolitionist, and Lovejoy was passionate in his devotion
to the Abolition cause, yet he made concessions to Mr. Lincoln's
policies such as William Lloyd Garrison, Wendell Phillips, Joshua R.
Giddings and other hotheaded zealots simply could or would not
make. Lovejoy knew that Lincoln hated slavery, that he was honest
and could be trusted, so he refrained from needling or embarrassing
Lincoln, both during the campaign of 1860, and when as President
the lonely man in the White House was wrestling with titanic
problems and hounded by relentless detractors.

Thus in a speech at Cooper Union, New York, Lovejoy said:

> The President is like a man driving a horse in the thills of a buggy
> and leading another behind by a halter-strap. It is very awkward manag-
> ing two horses this way, as I know from experiment. Now the Presi-
> dent knows that the horse Radical that he is driving can go ahead
> for he has by him been taken in handsome style into the Executive
> chair; but he is a little afraid that this mettlesome charger cannot be
> trusted going down hill, otherwise he would let go of the old rack of
> bones that hobbles along behind. Now I do not propose to dash ahead
> so as to throw the President out, or break the carriage, but to go so
> steadily, that the Executive can be assured that he is safe with the
> Radical steed, down hill as well as up, and on level ground. . . If the
> President does not believe all I do, I believe all he does. If he does not
> drive as fast as I would, he is on the same road, and it is a question
> of time.

This apt, quaint and lumbering illustration so readily understood
by those of the horse and buggy days, quite convincingly sets forth
the attitude of Lovejoy to the President. Very likely it infuriated
the other radical Abolitionists who couldn't understand and had no

sympathy with Lovejoy's temporizing with the President's policies and, apparently, supporting them with zest. If Lincoln was a statesman in taking his time to work out the grievous problems that were never absent from his office and seldom from his mind, Lovejoy was also a statesman in his refusal to prod the President into premature action. He too knew how to bide his time yet never ceasing in his fierce denunciations of the institution of slavery.

That Lovejoy was sometimes fanatically fervid in his attacks upon slavery is of course true. But is it just to call Lovejoy a fanatic? Many said he was. That he was a bitter and relentless foe of slavery is a fact. Even if he deserved the term of opprobrium, he was in good company. The world's reformers have usually been so stigmatized. They called Jesus a fanatic, or the equivalent. Owen Lovejoy could no more rid his memory of that awful night at Alton when his brother lay dead at his feet, than Saul of Tarsus could blot from his mind the memory of the scene when Stephen died a martyr's death—with this difference: some of the blood of Stephen was on the young rabbi's hands, while the blood of Elijah Lovejoy splotched the hands of the mob which took his life. Still, it is not quite accurate to describe Owen Lovejoy as a fanatic. Had he been fanatically minded would he have gone along with Abraham Lincoln so patiently, sympathetically, and loyally? For one, I doubt it. Fanatics are not so constituted. That vow Lovejoy took as he knelt by the side of his brother struck down by maddened defenders of slavery was ever fresh in his mind. Thus in a speech before a Republican caucus, he thundered: "There never was a more causeless revolt since Lucifer led his cohorts of apostate angels against the Throne of God, but I never heard that the Almighty proposed to compromise the matter by allowing the rebels to kindle the fires of hell south of the celestial meridian of 36° 30″." Nevertheless this preacher-congressman stood by Lincoln. The fair-mindedness of Lovejoy and his willingness to support Lincoln at all hazards made him quick to censure his fellow Abolitionists when he thought them biased and bitterly partisan.

Lovejoy made a fierce rejoinder to William Lloyd Garrison's attack on Lincoln in 1862, and to Thaddeus Stevens' proposals to treat the South as a conquered province, and he rebuked his colleagues in the spirit of the President's magnanimous reconstruction program. On the other hand he was charged by proslavery men as being unfriendly to the South, and in reply to such strictures said: "You speak of me as unfriendly to the South. I am even denounced as an enemy to my country. I hope you will believe that I love my country, and all my country. It is because I love my country with all my heart and soul that I am anxious to remove from her fair face this hideous deformity of human slavery."

A rare man was this preacher-statesman. A fierce fighter for the right as he saw it, he also had a gentler side. He was not without a sense of humor and relished a good story.

It was Lovejoy who figured in a famous tilt with the irritable Secretary of War, Edwin M. Stanton. A plan for mingling eastern and western troops was urged on Lincoln by a committee headed by Congressman Lovejoy. Lincoln sent a note by Lovejoy suggesting a transfer of regiments. Stanton's brow was black.

"Did Lincoln give you an order of that kind?" the bellicose Secretary asked.

"He did, sir," replied Lovejoy.

"Then he is a damned fool," thundered Stanton.

"Do you mean to say the President is a damned fool?"

"Yes, sir, if he gave you such an order as that."

In the President's office Lovejoy told what had occurred.

"Did Stanton say I was a damned fool?" Lincoln asked.

"He did, sir, and repeated it."

The President pondered the remark. "If Stanton said I was a damned fool, then I must be one, for he is nearly always right, and generally says what he means. I will step over and see him."

III

Owen Lovejoy's relation with Abraham Lincoln was as friend and counselor. Mr. Lincoln's intimates were never numerous, but this Congregational preacher-agitator was of the inner circle among the few intimate friends of Mr. Lincoln's political life. They corresponded freely, and Lovejoy was a welcome visitor to "The Executive Mansion," as Mr. Lincoln called it, at any time, night or day. To Frank B. Carpenter, the portrait painter who spent six months in the White House, Lincoln said: "Lovejoy was the best friend I had in Congress." When Lovejoy lay on his bed at Washington with the sickness from which he died, the President visited him repeatedly. On one of these visits Mr. Lincoln remarked with forebodings: "This war is eating my life out. I have a strong impression that I shall not live to see the end."

In what high and affectionate esteem did Preacher Lovejoy hold Abraham Lincoln? On April 24, 1862, Lovejoy answered this question in a speech in the House of Representatives. He said:

> I too have a niche for Abraham Lincoln, but it is in Freedom's holy fame and not in the blood-besmeared temple of human bondage; not surrounded by slave-fetters and chains, but radiant with the light of Liberty. In that niche he shall stand proudly, nobly, gloriously, with shattered fetters and broken chains and slave-whips beneath his feet. If Abraham Lincoln pursues the path evidently pointed out for him in the Providence of God, as I believe he will, then he will occupy the proud position I have indicated. That is a fame worth living for . . . aye more, that is a fame worth dying for, though that death led through the blood of Gethsemane and the agony of the accursed tree. . . . Let Abraham Lincoln make himself . . . the emancipator, the liberator . . . and his name shall not be enrolled in this earthly temple, but it will be traced on the living stones of that temple which rears itself amid the thrones and hierarchies of Heaven.

What must have been Abraham Lincoln's emotions when he read that speech made by his "generous friend," the Rev. Owen Lovejoy, Yankee come to Illinois!

Two years later as Lovejoy neared the end, his strong frame broken and weakened, he said to Frank B. Carpenter: "I tell you Mr. Lincoln is at heart as strong an antislavery man as any of them, but he is compelled to *feel* his way. He has a responsibility in this matter which many men do not seem to be able to comprehend. I say to you, frankly, that I believe his course is right. His mind acts slowly, but when he moves, it is *forward*."

So passed on another:

Who never turned his back but marched breast forward,
Never doubted clouds would break,
Never dreamed, though right were worsted, wrong would triumph;
Held we fall to rise, are baffled to fight better,
        Sleep to wake.

Chapter VII

The Reverend Benjamin H. Smith

He preached a sermon with Abraham Lincoln as the only auditor.

****

NOT many clergymen have preached a full-length sermon to a single hearer, but that is what the Rev. Benjamin H. Smith did, with Abraham Lincoln as the only hearer. The sermon was preached in Mr. Lincoln's Springfield office, and at his request. Before I come to this sermon, I am proud to relate that in a little Missouri town on a remarkable Sunday I made the "good confession," following a sermon by this same Benjamin H. Smith.

Dr. Smith was at that time president of Christian University, Canton, Missouri, and also president of a bank in that town on the banks of the Mississippi. These facts I did not know when I sat in the Christian Church in LaBelle, Lewis County, Missouri, that winter Sunday morning; nor did I so much as dream that this preacher had known Abraham Lincoln, and had preached a sermon to the Springfield lawyer in his law office there many years previous.

Dr. Smith was a man of impressive appearance, and a regal figure in the pulpit, with a great shock of graying hair and a closely cropped beard after the fashion of that day. An article by Simpson Ely in the *Central Christian Register* for July 26, 1900, gives us a picture of the man:

Among the Disciples of Christ in Missouri few men were more widely and more favorably known than Benjamin H. Smith, late of Canton, Mo. Indeed he had a national reputation, and an influence that could not be restricted to state lines. He departed this earthly life on the eleventh day of July, 1900, in the seventy-second year of his age, and after an illness that extended through five weary years. He lived for a little while "upon borrowed time," by reason of his strength; "yet was his strength labor and sorrow." He died, as he lived, a Christian, and in the triumphs of faith. On his last Lord's day on earth he sang one of Zion's songs and preached and exhorted those present. Death had no terrors for him. Thanks be to God who gave him the victory through our Lord Jesus Christ.

From whatever standpoint you judged Benjamin H. Smith, he was a giant. Physically he was a magnificent specimen of manhood. He was in height considerably over six feet and at his best weighed little less than three hundred pounds. He did not appear gross, but was finely proportioned. He would attract attention and command admiration in a crowd. He moved with a majestic tread, and was a prince among men. He was a born gentleman. No one who ever looked upon his face could forget it. His strong features impressed the beholder deeply. The massive and handsome forehead, the keen but kindly eyes looking out from beneath splendid eyebrows, the well-chiseled nose, the expressive mouth and the strong chin, could not be seen and then forgotten.

He had a mind worthy of its magnificent temple and a heart as big as his body. To splendid natural endowments he added an acquired culture that few others have possessed. He was a graduate of Bethany College, and he not only sat at the feet of "the Sage of Bethany" [1]; but he imbibed his spirit, acquired his faith in the Word of God, and imitated his loyalty to the cause of primitive, apostolic Christianity. That faith never failed him. It was the inspiration of his life, his solace in affliction and the ground of hope in his death.

For a time he engaged in the practice of law, but after his conversion he resolved to devote his God-given powers to the preaching of the Gospel, and many are the souls whom he led out of darkness into light, and out of despair into hope . . .

[1] *Author's note:* The renowned Alexander Campbell, who founded Bethany College in 1840.

I thought no President of the United States could outshine this preacher as I gazed upon him with something akin to awe. I am unable to recall the text of the sermon that morning, or a single illustration used . . . I only know something in the person of the speaker and his impassioned presentation of the righteousness of the Christian life led me to the front seat and a timid yet resolute confession of faith.

Some years later I read in one of our church papers an article of absorbing interest by Benjamin H. Smith, recounting his acquaintance with Mr. Lincoln and the sermon he had preached to him as he sat in a characteristic posture in his law office at Springfield. I meant to clip the article, but neglected to do so. Perhaps if I had cut the article out I'd have lost it somewhere along the way, for my student years were just ahead of me. As my interest in Lincoln lore greatened, I kept recalling the article by Rev. Smith, which I had read with avidity a quarter of a century before. I inquired of numerous Lincoln students if they knew of such an article, but they had not seen or heard of it. Then when I began to do research on the subject of Lincoln and the Preachers, I set about determined to find the Smith statement. I journeyed to St. Louis and spent hours going through the files of *The Christian Evangelist*, in which weekly I think it originally appeared, but in vain. Certain files for the early 1890's were not available, and the likelihood is that the Smith article appeared during that period.

Undaunted by my failure I next put a notice in *The Christian Evangelist* and *The Christian Standard* of Cincinnati, describing the article, and stating I greatly desired a copy. I had about despaired of success when lo! I received a letter from the Rev. J. M. Morris of California, enclosing the coveted composition, which he said he had clipped from a copy of *The Plow and Hammer*, a publication I had never heard of before. He informed me that he found the article somewhere around 1890, which fixed the date of its publication approximately. It is now my good fortune and pleasure to reproduce a fascinating document in Lincolniana, and one not generally known:

The Smith Statement

I was president of the Ladies Seminary at Bloomington, Illinois; I preached one-half the Sundays at Springfield. I often made my home over Sunday with Judge Logan, a law partner with Lincoln for many years. One Saturday afternoon I was walking down into the city with Judge Logan. He saw Mr. Lincoln coming down the street, meeting us. Judge Logan asked me, "Smith, have you met Lincoln?" I answered, "No." "Well, yonder he comes and I want you to meet him." And in a few minutes I was introduced to him. . . .

I heard Lincoln say as Logan started after me, "I will be there, Logan." Then it came to me that Lincoln was going to come out and hear me preach in the little church around the corner. And sure enough, he came on Sunday morning. I preached as best I could and administered the Lord's Supper and closed the services, after which Lincoln came forward and shook hands with me very cordially and said: "Elder Smith, I want some more of that teaching; I will come again."

He came to hear me that night and often after that. One Monday morning, as I went to the railroad depot, I met Lincoln. I found he was going away on the same train. But he said: "Elder, our train is two hours late. Come, go with me to my office." I accepted the invitation.

I took a new survey of the man as we walked along together. I was greatly impressed with his frank, homely expressions; his open countenance; and the broad tolerant spirit that he breathed through his sentences as we walked along. In those days our people [the Disciples] received but little recognition from dignitaries. Entering the door of his office Lincoln seated me in the best old-fashioned chair in the room, and then locked the door. "You see, Elder, I will make like I am not in. I want to hear you preach." He buried his face in his big bony hands, his elbows resting upon his knees and said: "Now, Elder, I want you to begin at A and go clear on down to Izzard. I want you to tell me the whole system of religion as taught by your people."

Well, I began and preached to Lincoln for one full hour, setting forth the plea that the Christian Church was making with the churches and the world to return to the ancient order of things. And Lincoln never moved or said a word. He said that he would not ask a question or bother me during the whole sermon. I never preached to such an appreciative audience before nor since. And when I was done, I said: "Now, Mr. Lincoln, if you have anything to say, say on."

He said, "Elder, that is all very plain. I like that. It is sensible. It all commends itself to the head and heart of any hearer."

Mr. Lincoln then introduced two stories, both of them having to do with a colored preacher. The second story ran like this: There was a darkey who wanted to join the church, and the preacher asked him if he understood the doctrine of predestination. The darkey said: "Yes, sah, if dah is anything I understands, sah, it am predisternation." The preacher remarked to him that before he could consistently take him in, he would have to ask him a few questions on that subject and satisfy himself that he was prepared to enter the church with orthodox views. So the preacher asked him a great many questions and finally asked the darkey if he now understood it all. The darkey replied: "Well, brudder, when you fust asked me, I knew all about it, but since you done splained it all out, I knos noffin about it at all."

Mr. Lincoln's application of the story was as follows: "Elder Smith, I understand your explanation of foreordination, election and predestination; I understand your plea for a return to the apostolic order of things religious; but the way preachers have generally explained these things, the more they explained the less I understood them, and my mind got more and more muddled. And, I must confess that the latter story sometimes expresses a state of my mind that to me is dangerous. The preachers have preached and talked this "miraculous conversion," and such other, to me, very absurd theories of religion, and given such contradictory explanations of the Bible, that I have honestly at times doubted the whole thing."

Thus endeth the lesson and it is, I hold, one to remember and to cherish. For one thing it reveals the easy friendly connection which Mr. Lincoln had with his preacher associates. For another, it supplies a new Lincoln story, not at all easy to turn up these days. Then too, and perhaps this is most important, it reveals Lincoln's interest in religion together with a frank confession of his intellectual difficulties with some of the speculative and contradictory theology which appeared in much of the preaching of his times.

Is it strange, or a small matter, that I treasure the memory of the Rev. Dr. Benjamin H. Smith, silk hat, gold-headed cane, and his very great kindness to a small boy who found the "way of the life everlasting" under his able preaching?

Chapter VIII

Two Militant Controversialists:
Archbishop Hughes and the
Reverend Dr. Breckinridge

Both stood for the Union and President Lincoln

****

ARCHBISHOP John J. Hughes (1797-1864) of New York, and the Rev. Dr. Robert J. Breckinridge (1800-1871) of Kentucky, were distinguished servants of the Most High, who battled for the Lord and Abraham Lincoln. Differing in background and in church affiliations, these two ecclesiastics had in common three things, namely: they possessed great natural ability together with unique gifts as controversialists, and they were alike sturdy and articulate defenders of the Federal Union.

Archbishop Hughes was born in Ireland of humble and devout parentage; Dr. Breckinridge came from one of Kentucky's first families, and was a bluestocking Presbyterian, in short, an aristocrat. The Archbishop was fairly well educated but not highly so; Dr. Breckinridge was a classical scholar, and a superbly trained theologian. Both men were stalwart defenders of the truth as they saw it, and both wrote and spoke clear, effective, and eloquent English. Archbishop Hughes was the widely recognized spokesman for the Catholic church in America, and Dr. Breckinridge's name was known from coast to coast as a Protestant champion.

Both of these churchmen were pamphleteers, and took to the printed page with gusto. In literary output, however, the Presbyterian polemic outdistanced his Roman Catholic contemporary. One of the Kentuckian's biographers wrote: "A complete collection of Dr. Breckinridge's books, debates, articles, and pamphlets on slavery, temperance, popery, universalism, education, agriculture and politics would form a five-foot shelf of books."

Each of these ecclesiastical gladiators took to the arena ripe for the fray whenever the cause they loved was assailed, and neither asked for nor gave quarter to the foe. Thus the Archbishop while still a college student replied to a criticism of the Catholic church made by a Fourth of July orator in an address in Chambersburg, Pennsylvania, which was published in a local paper. From then on to the end of his days this Catholic prelate was on the firing line defending his church on the Public School Question, The Native American Movement, and scores of other controversial subjects. One of Dr. Hughes' liveliest debates was with Dr. John Breckinridge, an older brother of Robert J., who preceded the latter in the pastorate of the Second Presbyterian Church of Baltimore.

In Protestant controversial circles, the reputation of Dr. R. J. Breckinridge was fully as strong as the Archbishop's, and his fight in what was known among Presbyterians as the "Act and Testimony" issue of 1834, which was led by him, resulted in a division of the Presbyterian church into the "Old" and "New" schools, otherwise known as conservative and liberal. Breckinridge was squarely aligned with the first-named group.

A year prior to this split the Synod of Kentucky discussed for two days, with much spirit, an overture which declared slavery as existing within its bounds, a great moral evil and inconsistent with the Word of God. The Synod was much divided upon the question, and the subject was indefinitely postponed. At that juncture Breckinridge left the house saying, "Since God has forsaken the Synod of Kentucky, Robert J. Breckinridge will forsake it too."

Now that we have a fairly good picture of these two protagonists, it is time to see the part they played in the stark drama of the Civil War, and their relation to President Abraham Lincoln.

I

Most of the great Irish Catholic leaders, such as Daniel O'Connell and Father Matthew, were foes of Negro slavery, and Archbishop Hughes was no exception. But his Grace was not an Abolitionist, and in the earlier stages of the "irrepressible conflict," he cautioned patience and diplomacy. He was annoyed when Daniel O'Connell, Father Matthew and other antislavery Irishmen published an address which the Abolitionists hastened to use in behalf of their cause. In reply, the Archbishop published a statement in which he said: "I am no friend to slavery, but I am still less friendly to any attempt of foreign origin to abolish it." This was 1842, and the churchman pretty fairly mirrored in his statement the minds of many Americans who later stood by the Union when the test came.

Hughes was a long-time friend of Governor William H. Seward, and when he became Secretary of State, the correspondence between the two was extensive; moreover, it was of such importance that the secretary often passed the Archbishop's letters to the President, who read them with interest.

In 1861, under date of October 21, President Lincoln wrote Archbishop Hughes as follows:

> Rt. Rev. Sir: I am sure you will pardon me if, in my ignorance, I do not address you with technical correctness.
>
> I find no law authorizing the appointment of chaplains for our *hospitals*; and yet the services of chaplains are more needed, perhaps in the hospitals, than by the healthy soldiers in the field. With this in view, I have given a sort of *quasi* appointment (a copy of which I enclose) to each of the three Protestant ministers, who have accepted, and entered upon their duties.
>
> If you perceive no objections, I will thank you to give me the name,

or names, of one or more suitable persons of the Catholic Church, to whom I may with propriety tender the same service.

Many thanks for your kind and judicious letters to Gov. Seward, and which he regularly allows me the pleasure and profit of perusing.

With the highest respect, your obedient servant.

A. LINCOLN.

This letter deserves an observation or two. It reveals faultlessly the unaffected humility of the President, and it is couched in gracious terms. Likewise, it indicates the high esteem in which Lincoln held this Irish-born prelate who rose to great heights in his church and in the nation. For a third thing, this letter is further proof, if indeed any were needed, of the President's complete freedom from creedal prejudice.

On the same day the President wrote Archbishop Hughes, Secretary Seward invited him to Washington for a private conference. This was a few days after Messrs. Mason and Slidell, Confederate commissioners to England and France, had succeeded in running the blockade from Charleston, intending to take passage to Europe at Havana. The administration decided to counteract this action by sending envoys who would be free from the restraints of diplomatic etiquette, and determined to send Archbishop Hughes to France and Thurlow Weed to England. It was with reference to this appointment that the Archbishop was called to Washington. In a letter written later to Cardinal Barnabo, Prefect of the Sacred Congregation of the Propaganda, the Archbishop said:

It was proposed by the cabinet that I should accept a special mission to England and France in connection with very important national questions between the United States and these powers. I declined until it was made known to me that the President of the United States made it a special request that I accept, and if possible render some service to the United States in the present condition of public affairs. . . . I could not refuse this request, and at the same time I imagined if any success should attend my mission, it would redound to the benefit of the Catholics, and to the promotion of the interests of the church.

Archbishop Hughes spent eight months in Europe, during which time he interviewed the French emperor, attended a canonization of martyrs in Rome, laid the cornerstone of a new Catholic university in Dublin, saw the Holy Father, and put in a good word, wherever possible and prudent, for the preservation of the Union and the success of the armies of the North. His letters to Secretary Seward, written from various points in Europe, make interesting reading in his biography by John R. G. Hassard, published in 1866.

On the Archbishop's return to this country in 1862, he preached a sermon in the Cathedral in New York to a crowded audience. In the course of the sermon he commended the President's calling for a draft of six hundred thousand men, and said:

> If I had a voice in the councils of the country, I would say let volunteering continue; if the 300,000 on your list be not enough this week, next week make a draft of 300,000 more. It is not cruel, this. This is mercy; this is humanity. Anything that will put an end to this drenching with blood the whole surface of the country, that will be humanity. . . It is not necessary to hate our enemies; it is not necessary to be cruel in battle, nor be cruel after its termination. It is necessary to be true, to be patriotic, to do for the country what the country needs, and the blessing of God will recompense those who discharge their duty without faltering, and without violating any of the laws of God or man.

This sermon was criticized by Catholics in the South, but the Archbishop stood by his guns.

The Archbishop had been ailing for some months, and active almost to the last, he died on Sunday evening, January 3, 1864, aged sixty-seven years. The church he had served so faithfully and the nation for the unity of which he had prayed and labored alike paid him homage. The Irish farm boy had risen to great heights of fame and power in the new land of his adoption.

II

Down in Kentucky Dr. Robert J. Breckinridge was fighting on several fronts and enjoying it hugely—writing books; making speeches in behalf of temperance and against what he termed "Popery"; editing a militant weekly journal; preaching and shepherding the flock, occupying a chair in theology; superintending the public schools of Kentucky. Yes sir, the old Doctor was a busy man. But not too busy to lay off fighting slavery for a single day, or to falter for an instant in assailing an ominous thing which some called "Secession," but branded by him as rebellion.

Kentucky was dividing over the issues of states' rights and the institution of Negro slavery. Feeling was intense, passions hot, and the Doctor's own family was divided; but no matter how painful it was for him, Robert J. stood by his colors, which in this instance was the flag of the Union. Lexington was largely proslavery and with a few exceptions the best families were joining up with the Confederacy. The Doctor put on his shining armor, in this case, his best broadcloth coat, high hat—but no gloves—and went into action. He began with his own family, and to one of his sons wrote:

> I am utterly opposed and will resist to the uttermost of my ability, a confederacy of the fifteen states—deeming such a result the most fatal issue for Kentucky that the terrible condition of things admit of. Show this letter to Robert, and let me earnestly beseech you both not to take a single step, even the smallest, that can by any possibility conduct you into the direction of disunion. The whole thing is utter madness, and the pretexts for it are futile, some false, some atrocious; not one of them such as becomes a statesman, a philosopher, a patriot or a Christian; not one of them will endure the light of history, the judgment of mankind, or the scrutiny of posterity.

The old Doctor knew the power of words, and particularly the *right* word, in the choice of which he was a connoisseur.

Abraham Lincoln had heard, and may have met, Dr. Breckinridge when as congressman-elect he visited Lexington with his family in 1847. He spent three weeks in his wife's home town enjoying what was perhaps the first real vacation he had known. On Thanksgiving Day, Congressman Lincoln was privileged to hear the great Doctor Breckinridge preach. Very likely Mary Todd Lincoln sat by his side in the pew as the "plumed crusader of the Cross" as William H. Townsend of Lexington named him, preached with lucidity, conviction, and tremendous vigor. Lincoln knew where this man stood on the issues destined to divide the nation that were already forming, but not in his wildest dreams could he imagine that the old Doctor would some day come to his aid to save Kentucky for the Union.

And now the war had come to the nation, and to Kentucky where the division was close and tense and pain wrought. The Doctor's family was divided; his nephew, a son-in-law and two of his sons had gone over to the South and were in uniforms of gray. The iron entered the preacher-patriot's soul, but he stood by and fought for the Union, no matter his personal sorrows. . . . The early successes of the Southern army dismayed but did not discourage the old warrior, and he set himself resolutely to keep Kentucky from seceding to the Confederacy. So he fought on with pen and voice, his slogan: "Kentucky stand by the Union!"

At Washington Abraham Lincoln knew he had a friend in Lexington that nothing could swerve from support of the Union cause. The Presidential election of 1864 was in the offing, and political enemies were putting new furrows in the haggard face of the tall gaunt man in the White House. At such a trying time a "white Knight" came to Lincoln's aid. Dr. Breckinridge was chosen as a delegate to the National Union Convention which convened in Baltimore. On the 7th of June, 1864, that convention was called to order by Senator Morgan, who in a brief speech announced that Dr. Robert J. Breckinridge had been chosen temporary chairman. Amid thunderous applause the delegates greeted the sixty-four-year-old crusader. He was an impressive person. His "white grizzly hair parting almost from his brows, thin face, and long pointed beard," with a resonant voice to command a listening senate or a noisy convention, he looked the man of strength and conviction that he was. The old Doctor began in low mellow tones, clear, forceful, rising in volume until his voice filled the hall. In the course of his speech he rose far above partisan or sectional politics when he declared:

> As a Union man I will follow you to the ends of the earth and to the gates of death, but as an Abolition Party, as a Republican Party, as a Whig Party, as a Democratic Party, I will not follow you one foot. . . I know very well that the sentiments I am uttering will cause a great odium in the state in which I was born, which I love, where the bones of two generations of my ancestors, and some of my children are, and where soon I shall lay my own. I know very well that my colleagues will incur odium if they endorse what I say, and they too, know it. But [and here he raised his arms high above his head and spoke with a firm, slow ringing emphasis] we have put our faces toward the way in which we intend to go, and we will go in it to the end.

In an impassioned passage the great old Doctor poured forth a pellucid stream of powerful oratory, in which he castigated unmercifully the "traitors," as he called his friends and neighbors who had gone over to the Confederacy. He thundered: "No government has ever been built upon imperishable foundations which were not laid in the blood of traitors. It is a fearful truth, but we had as well avow it at once. Every blow you strike, and every rebel you kill, every battle you win, dreadful as it is to do it, you are adding, in may be a year, it may be a century, or ten centuries to the life of the government and the freedom of your children."

Commenting on this speech, William H. Townsend in his book *Lincoln and His Wife's Home Town*, writes: "The delegates sat as if stunned by the very intensity of his utterance. Friends of many years who knew that the old patriot had a 'rebel' nephew and two 'rebel' sons whom he loved better than life, found their eyes blurred with tears as he struggled to control his emotions, and then continued."

The day following this speech, Breckinridge was in Washington with the committee to notify Lincoln of his nomination, and on Sunday, June 12th, he preached in the Hall of Representatives "a pure gospel sermon and very able." So Senator Orville Hickman Browning wrote in his diary. We wish we knew the text, and would prize a transcript of the sermon Dr. Breckinridge preached on that notable occasion.

Robert Jefferson Breckinridge was in truth a great man; great in quality of mind; great in courage; great in convictions; great in golden speech; great in patriotic ardor; great in most things that make human beings only a little lower than God. Without this preacher of the Everlasting Gospel and defender of the Union, it is doubtful of Abraham Lincoln could have held Kentucky in line, and had that state gone over to the Confederacy, Missouri and other border states might have done likewise. That would have meant a longer, more costly and bloodier war; but the old Doctor held the fort, and his fidelity, sincerity and courage endeared him even to those who gave their all to "the Lost Cause."

> Unawed By Opinion,
> Unseduced By Flattery,
> Undismayed By Disaster
> He Confronted Life With Antique Courage
> And Death With Christian Hope.

These two ardent controversialists—Archbishop John Joseph Hughes and the Rev. Dr. Robert Jefferson Breckinridge—have been in their graves the better part of a century. Their lives were filled with battles, and they sleep well!

Chapter IX

Henry Ward Beecher:
The Shakespeare of the Pulpit

He was to Lincoln what Aaron was to Moses.

✳✳✳✳✳✳✳✳✳✳✳✳✳✳✳✳✳✳✳✳✳✳✳✳✳✳✳✳✳✳✳✳✳✳✳✳✳

O N THE twenty-sixth day of February, 1860, Abraham Lincoln went to Plymouth Church, Brooklyn, to hear Henry Ward Beecher preach. He had come to New York to make a political address which was originally set for delivery in Plymouth Church, but was changed and perhaps wisely, to the Cooper Union, which was more centrally located. The tall angular lawyer from Springfield, Illinois, according to one account, took an inconspicuous seat in the balcony, was recognized and escorted to pew 89, downstairs and well up front to the right of the pulpit.

Mr. Lincoln knew Beecher by reputation[1] . . . and who did not? The Illinoisan was an omnivorous reader of the newspapers, and no public man of his day was more constantly publicized than this

[1] The story of Lincoln in disguise visiting Beecher at his Brooklyn home at night, where the two men sank to their knees in prayer, is probably apocryphal. Beecher never mentioned it, and Mrs. Beecher recalled long after it happened, a tall man coming late at night, seeking out her husband for prayer and spiritual solace. If it did happen, it is curious that no confirmations came at the time, or shortly after the President's passing. It is hard to believe that at such a time of national peril the President could slip away from Washington, go to Brooklyn, and return without his aides knowing anything about it. Or, if they knew, would not have told about it immediately following Mr. Lincoln's death.

Brooklyn preacher. Then too, Lincoln's law partner, William H. Herndon, was interested in Beecher, and in the habit of passing on to the senior member of the firm sermons by Beecher. So Lincoln settled himself in the pew and awaited with no small eagerness the sermon of the morning.

Beecher was forty-seven years old at the time; his brown hair just touched with gray hung in curling ringlets about his neck and coat collar. His full round cherubic face was unlined by care and sorrow. His figure, destined later to be corpulent, was plump but not fat. He was in his magnificent middle life, the Shakespeare of the Pulpit, internationally known for his eloquent oratory, unconventional manner, and courage to speak out on the red-hot issues of his day, both theological and political. While not fully siding with the Abolitionists, he was an outright and bitter foe of slavery. A son of Old Lyman Beecher, who was a born polemic, brother of Harriet Beecher Stowe, whose *Uncle Tom's Cabin* had found an immense audience, Henry Ward Beecher was the best known of American preachers, and Sunday after Sunday packed Plymouth Church to the doors, often turning away disappointed multitudes.

We know what Beecher preached on that memorable Sunday morning. His text was Colossians 2:6-10, a lengthy passage from which the pastor of Plymouth's flock preached a full hour. The sermon in its entirety appears in Appendix II in this volume, and it is as fresh and stimulating as though preached only yesterday. This preacher didn't know how to be dull. He played upon his throngs of hearers as a master musician performs upon his favorite instrument.

In his *Six Months in the White House with Abraham Lincoln*,[2] F. B. Carpenter writes:

> Mr. Nelson Sizer, one of the gallery ushers of Henry Ward Beecher's church in Brooklyn, told me that about the time of the Cooper Insti-

[2] New York: Hurd & Houghton, Publishers, 1867, p. 135.

tute speech, Mr. Lincoln was twice present at the morning services of that church. On the first occasion, he was accompanied by his friend, George B. Lincoln, Esq., and occupied a prominent seat in the center of the house. On a subsequent Sunday morning, not long afterward, the church was packed, as usual, and the services had proceeded to the announcement of the text, when the gallery door at the right of the organ loft opened, and the tall figure of Mr. Lincoln entered, alone. Again in the city over Sunday, he started out by himself to find the church which he reached considerably behind time. Every seat was occupied; but the gentlemanly usher at once surrendered his own, and stepping back, became much interested in watching the effect of the sermon upon the western orator. As Mr. Beecher developed his line of argument, Mr. Lincoln's body swayed forward, his lips parted, and he seemed at length entirely unconscious of his surroundings—frequently giving vent to his satisfaction, at a well-put point or illustration, with a kind of involuntary Indian exclamation, "ugh," not audible beyond his immediate presence, but very expressive! Mr. Lincoln henceforward had a profound admiration for the talents of the famous pastor of Plymouth Church.

The date of this second visit of Mr. Lincoln to Plymouth Church was March 11, 1860, and the text of the sermon was Hebrews XI:13-16:

> These all died in faith, not having received the promises, but having seen them afar off, and were persuaded of them, and embraced them, and confessed that they were strangers and pilgrims on the earth. For they that say such things declare plainly that they seek a country. And truly, if they had been mindful of that country from whence they came out, they might have had opportunity to have returned. But now they desire a better country, that is, an heavenly: wherefore God is not ashamed to be called their God; for he hath prepared for them a city.

I

The names of Abraham Lincoln and Henry Ward Beecher are linked together in the story of that bloody conflict that deserves to be called "the great American tragedy." Actually, these two men were not well acquainted. Writing in Allen Thorndyke Rice's *Reminiscences of Abraham Lincoln, By Distinguished Men of His Time,* Beecher says: "My acquaintance with Lincoln can hardly be called an acquaintance. I was rather an observer." He then goes on to describe a call which he made upon the President in 1864: "We were alone in the receiving room. His hair was 'every way for Sunday'; it looked as though it was an abandoned stubblefield. He had on slippers, and his vest was what was called 'going free' . . . I do not know that I ever saw him after that."

No, Beecher never saw Lincoln after that, but both Lincoln and Beecher kept in communication with each other, and one of the President's last acts before the fatal Friday of April 14, 1865, was to appoint Henry Ward to make the oration at the raising of the flag over Fort Sumter as the Union army took over. And of all the noble tributes paid Abraham Lincoln by contemporary orators, Beecher's, delivered April 23rd in Plymouth Church on "The Effect of the Death of Lincoln," stands unrivaled in strength, beauty and sublimity of phrasings.

At first Beecher's support of Lincoln was little more than lukewarm. The Brooklyn orator wanted action, and the President wisely was biding his time. Why did not he free the slaves at once? Beecher wondered, and put his wonderment in public speech. Lincoln knew why, and was silent for the time. As editor of *The Independent,* Henry Ward reached an audience of millions, and on July 10, 1862, he wrote editorially:

> This is the common people's war; they furnish the men, the money, and its enthusiasm and patriotism. They can understand war. . . What has Mr. Lincoln's education done for him—more than ours for us—to fit him to judge military affairs? We are sick and weary of this conduct. We have a sacred cause, a noble army, good officers and heroic common people, but we are like to be ruined by an administration that will not tell the truth; that spends precious time at president-

making; that is cutting and shuffling the cards for the next great political campaign.

There was probably not another eminent preacher in the United States at that time who would have cared to use in print or speech the reference in the above passage to a card game, but this preacher didn't hesitate to do so. Beecher went even farther in his criticism of the President, when on August 7, 1862, he volleyed:

Certainly neither Mr. Lincoln nor his cabinet have proven leaders. Fear was stronger than Faith. . . And never was a time when men's prayers so fervently asked God for a leader! He has refused our petition! . . . not a spark of genius has he [Lincoln]; not an element for leadership, not one particle of heroic enthusiasm. . . We must cease looking any more to Government; we must turn to ourselves. And the time may be here when the people will be called to act with a courage beyond all precedent. After . . . reverses have come and our rulers are fugitives from the proud Capitol, should they deem the task of maintaining the sanctity and integrity of the National Soil hopeless, then this Great People . . . may yet be called to take up the despairing work and carry it to victory.

Pretty drastic? Yes, but the general course of criticism of Lincoln and his administration was of this character: within his own party, not to speak of the Democratic opposition, Beecher had a knack of mirroring in speech and in print mass opinion quite accurately, and again on other occasions of running squarely against it when he was so disposed.

II

First and last Lincoln did Beecher favors that cannot be denied. For instance in Plymouth Church the Howard family stood high and close to Henry Ward. John Tasker Howard was one of the triumvirate, with Henry C. Bowen and David Hale, who founded Plymouth Church. John R. Howard, who married a Raymond, another prominent family in Plymouth Church, wrote a life of Henry Ward Beecher, published in 1891, four years after the renowned preacher-orator's death. On May 18, 1864, Joseph Howard, Jr.,[3] son of John R., forged an executive proclamation calling for the draft of four hundred thousand additional soldiers, and appointing a day of fasting and prayer. Paxton Hibben in his account of this serious affair says: "The moment was well seized to produce panic on the stock exchange upon which Howard counted." Hibben is not a friendly biographer of Beecher and his associates, but in this instance his observation was probably correct. Anyhow this was serious business; Howard was arrested and imprisoned in Fort Layfayette. Straightway Henry Ward Beecher made a trip to Washington to intercede with Lincoln for the release of the son of his most intimate friends. It was not an easy request to make, or to grant, but the hard-pressed, amiable President wrote a note to Secretary Stanton in which he said: "I very much wish to oblige Henry Ward Beecher." And he did "oblige" him, for Howard was released. If this incident proves anything, it is that Henry Ward stood high in Lincoln's estimation.

It is but fair that we hear Beecher's side of this sordid episode. Writing to John D. Defrees on August 2, 1864, Beecher said:

> I feel earnestly desirous that this lesson should turn to young Howard's moral benefit. He needed some such prostration, and I am glad to perceive that the sting of his punishment is the implication of a *treasonable* intent. He was the tool of a man who turned state's evidence and escaped; Joe had only the hope of making some money by a stock broker; he had not the foresight . . . enough to perceive the relations of his act to the Public Welfare. You must excuse my earnestness. He has been brought up in my parish under my eye, and is the *only* spotted child in a large family.

[3] Joe Howard was one of the most facile, reckless, rollicking, cynical and witty journalists in New York . . . Joe got top prices for his work—ten or twelve thousand a year—William A. Croffut, *An American Procession* (Boston: Little, Brown & Co., 1931), p. 264.

On August 3, 1864, John D. Defrees wrote to John Hay, sending Beecher's letter and asking that it be brought to Lincoln's attention. "The public," writes Defrees, "does not require the further punishment of Howard—the mere tool of speculating scoundrels—and his release will gratify many true friends. The President has no truer or better friend than Beecher, and I do trust he may be gratified in a matter which he has taken so much at heart."

This correspondence puts the issue in a softer light and reveals too, the shepherding heart of Henry Ward Beecher.

III

Henry Ward Beecher's visit to England in 1863, and his speeches in behalf of the Union Cause, have been variously appraised. Beecher's friends hailed his trip as a great and distinctive service to President Lincoln and the Union. Paxton Hibben scoffs at the claim that Beecher turned the tide of public sentiment Unionward by his oratorical triumphs in England. Professor Adams in his two-volume history of *Great Britain and the Civil War*, says in a footnote that there was no "crisis of opinion" in 1863, "but that the majority in each audience was friendly to him [Beecher]." That may be true, but to read Beecher's speeches at Manchester and Liverpool, as they were taken down stenographically, interruptions, catcalls and hisses and the like included, one is not so sure about the "friendly" nature of a big section of the audience. Here follows a transcript of Beecher's turbulent speech at Liverpool. The orator is in the midst of the beheckled delivery. There he stands, putting all his mighty oratorical resources into play, and not having an easy time of it. Hearken:

> . . . And now in the future it is the work of every good man and patriot not to create divisions, but to do the things that will make for peace. ("Oh, oh!" and laughter.) On our part it shall be done. (Applause and hisses, and "No, no!") On your part it ought to be done; and when in any of the convulsions that come upon the world Great

Britain finds herself struggling single-handed against the gigantic powers that spread oppression and darkness—(Applause, hisses and uproar)—there ought to be such cordiality that she can turn and say to her first-born and most illustrious child, "Come!" ("Hear, hear!"— applause, tremendous cheers and uproar.) I will not say that England cannot again, as hitherto, single-handed manage any power—(Applause and uproar)—but I will say that England and America together for religion and liberty—(A voice: "Soap, soap"—uproar and great applause)—are a match for the world. (Applause; a voice: "They don't want any more soft soap.") Now, gentlemen and ladies—(A voice: "Sam Slick!"; and another voice: "Ladies and gentlemen, if you please")—when I came I was asked whether I would answer questions, and I very readily consented to do so, as I had in other places; but I will tell you it was because I expected to have the opportunity of speaking with some sort of ease and quiet. (A voice: "So you have.") I have for an hour and a half spoken against a storm—("Hear, hear!") —and you yourselves are witnesses that, by the interruptions, I have been obliged to strive with my voice, so that I no longer have the power to control this assembly. (Applause.) And although I am in spirit perfectly willing to answer any question, and more than glad of the chance, yet I am by this very unnecessary opposition tonight incapacitated physically from doing it. Ladies and gentlemen, I bid you good evening.

For one, I think the Brooklyn preacher gave a sturdy account of himself in this series, and did the cause of the Union great good.[4]

IV

On April 14, 1865, the Stars and Stripes were raised again over Fort Sumter, and the orator of the day selected by the President for the memorable occasion was Henry Ward Beecher. The Shakespeare of the Pulpit was thoroughly prepared and at his best. It was

[4] Grant's victory at Vicksburg and Lee's defeat at Gettysburg made Beecher's efforts more effective than otherwise they could have been. Beecher's speeches became the talk of the London clubs, a sure sign of fame in the British Isles— Lyman Beecher Stowe, *Saints, Sinners and Beechers* (New York: Bobbs-Merrill Co., 1934).

the kind of an event he loved—history was being made. The scene was rainbowed with the dramatic, and a nation would follow him when the oration appeared the next day in the Northern newspapers. "He stood on a heap of stones," writes Paxton Hibben, "his slightly graying hair flying in the wind, his face flushed by the southern sun, his sonorous words echoing back from the battered walls." He began slowly, solemnly, with his spirit of exultation subdued:

Ladies and Gentlemen: On this solemn and joyful day, we again lift to the breeze our fathers' flag, now again the banner of the *United States*, with the fervent prayer that God would crown it with honor, protect it from treason, and send it down to our children, with all the blessings of civilization, liberty, and religion. Terrible in battle, may it be beneficent in peace. Happily, no bird or beast of prey has been inscribed upon it. The stars that redeem the night from darkness, and the beams of red light that beautify the morning, have been united upon its folds. As long as the sun endures, or the stars, may it wave over a nation neither enslaved nor enslaving. Once, and but once, has treason dishonored it. In that insane hour, when the guiltiest and bloodiest rebellion of time hurled its fires upon this fort, you sir, [turning to General Anderson] and a small heroic band, stood within these now crumbled walls, and did gallant and just battle for the honor and defense of the nation's banner.

The orator's physical being seemed to expand . . . his voice rose clear and vibrant as he declared:

We exult, not for a passion gratified, but for a sentiment victorious; not for temper, but for conscience; not as we devoutly believe that our will is done, but that God's will hath been done. We should be unworthy of that liberty entrusted to our care, if, on such a day as this, we sullied our hearts by feelings of aimless vengeance; and equally unworthy, if we did not devoutly thank Him who hath said, *Vengeance is mine, I will repay, saith the Lord*, that He hath set a mark upon arrogant rebellion, ineffaceable while time lasts!

. . . Long night has ended! And for this returning day we have come from afar, to rejoice and give thanks. No more war! No more

accursed secession! No more slavery, that spawned them both! . . .
In the name of God, we life up our banner, and dedicate it to peace,
union and liberty, now and forevermore. Amen.

It was a powerful speech, although Lincoln could not so have
spoken, for his heart was full of forgiveness, and he yearned for
complete reunion; but he chose the man who would be worthy the
event, and oratorically, Beecher was the man of that hour.

The day which began so joyously for the Union hosts at Charleston, ended in shadows . . . the President had been assassinated! The
dreadful word reached Beecher and his party, which included Theodore Tilton, the Rev. Dr. Richard S. Storrs, William Lloyd Garrison
and others, before they left Charleston, turning their elation into
sorrow. Arriving in New York Beecher went at once to Peekskill,
his country home, and began preparation for a funeral eulogy which
has not been surpassed in the annals of American oratory.

Sunday morning, April 23rd, nine days after Lincoln's passing,
the Shakespeare of the Pulpit preached in Plymouth Church on
"The Effect of the Death of Lincoln," with the text in Deuteronomy
34:1-5, the brief account of how Moses was led by the Lord to the
top of Mount Pisgah, whence he viewed the promised land into
which he might not enter. Plymouth Church was packed, and many
hundreds were turned away. Beecher's sensitive being was at concert
pitch. He met the occasion with an eloquence which even for him
was superb. With pictorial imagery and short vivid sentences inter-
spersed with longer ones, he described the effect of the assassination
of the President upon the people of the nation, doubting at first
that they could believe their eyes or ears, that Lincoln was dead.
Thus:

The blow brought not a sharp pang. It was so terrible that at first
it stunned sensibility. Citizens were like men awakened at midnight by
an earthquake and bewildered to find everything that they were accus-
tomed to trust wavering and falling. The very earth was no longer

solid. The first feeling was the least. Men waited to get straight to feel. They wandered in the streets as if groping after some impending dread, or undeveloped sorrow, or someone to tell them what ailed them. They met each other as if each would ask the other, "Am I awake, or do I dream?" There was a piteous helplessness. Strong men bowed down and wept. Other and common griefs belonged to someone in chief; this belonged to all. It was each and every man's. Every virtuous household in the land felt as if its firstborn were gone. Men were bereaved and walked for days as if a corpse lay unburied in their dwellings. There was nothing else to think of. They could speak of nothing but that; and yet of that they could speak only falteringly. All business was laid aside. Pleasure forgot to smile. The city for nearly a week ceased to roar. The great leviathan lay down, and was still. Even avarice stood still, and greed was strangely moved to generous sympathy and universal sorrow.

And now, the orator fully aroused, "shaking his invincible locks," declaims: "Rear to his name monuments, found charitable institutions and write his name above their lintels; but no monument will ever equal the universal, spontaneous and sublime sorrow that in a moment swept down lines and parties, and covered up animosities, and in an hour brought a divided people into unity of grief."

The sustained beatuy of diction and the near biblical grandeur of the vivid imagery required a majestic peroration, and Beecher was equal to it. The vast congregation sat silent save for subdued sobbing here and there as the orator reached his climax:

Dead, dead, dead, he yet speaketh. Is Washington dead? Is Hampden dead? Is David dead? Is any man that ever was fit to live dead? Disenthralled of flesh, and risen in the unobstructed sphere where passion never comes, he begins his illimitable work. His life now is grafted upon the infinite, and will be fruitful as no earthly life can be. Pass on, thou that hast overcome. Your sorrows, O people, are his peace. Your bells and bands and muffled drums sound triumph in his ear. Wail and weep here; God made it echo joy and triumph there. Pass on.

Four years ago, O Illinois, we took from your midst an untried man and from among the people. We return him to you a mighty conqueror. Not thine any more, but the nation's; not ours, but the world's. Give him place, O ye prairies. In the midst of this great continent his dust shall rest, a sacred treasure to myriads who shall pilgrim to that shrine to kindle anew their zeal and patriotism. Ye winds that move over the mighty places of the west, chant his requiem. Ye peoples, behold a martyr whose blood, as so many articulate words, pleads for fidelity, for law, for liberty.

If Henry Ward Beecher had done nothing else to bring him into the Lincoln drama, this distinctive specimen of noble funeral oratory, would have linked the names of Lincoln and Beecher for all times.

The Shakespeare of the Pulpit preached in Plymouth Church on Sunday evening, February 27, 1888. He spoke with vigor and was as exuberant of speech as ever. No one who heard him that evening imagined it was his last sermon; but it was. Following the service, and after asking the organist and choir to play and sing something for two little urchins, boy and girl, who had wandered from the streets into the church, attracted no doubt, by the bright lights and the music, Beecher went home to die. His death was the occasion of myriad tributes from the press and platform. Fifty thousand people representing many creeds and from every stratum of society passed in steady stream to look upon the well-known face.

The Shakespeare of the Pulpit had finished his exciting course, and the nation mourned.

Chapter X

The Tribute of the Synagogue

Being also some account of Lincoln and the Jews.

****

A MONG the ardent panegyrists of Abraham Lincoln, and they are myriad, few equal and none surpass in fervid adulation America's eloquent rabbis. Students of Lincoln are sometimes asked if there are not dissenting voices in the hallelujah chorus proclaiming him as "our First American," and the answer is, "Yes, an infinitesimal few, and not a single Jewish dissenter in the list." Pretty much like the rest of us, Jewish leaders revere Washington; honor Jefferson; toast Franklin; admire Hamilton; think highly of Jackson, "Old Hickory"; are fond of "T.R."; laud Wilson; blow hot and cold over "F.D.R."; but they *love* Lincoln!

I

The affection of the Jews for Lincoln and the manner in which they have enshrined his memory is the motif of this chapter, but some account of the Jews in the United States prior to Mr. Lincoln's Presidency is appropriate at this point. The best authority on Lincoln and the Jews is Dr. Isaac Markens, distinguished Jewish scholar, author and historian, who wrote among other works, *The Hebrews in America*. In his monograph on *Lincoln and the Jews*, now scarce and a rarity, Dr. Markens says: "The Jews of the United States formed but a small portion of the population in Lincoln's time. The president of the Board of Delegates of American Israelites, their representative organization, estimated their number in the loyal states near the close of 1861 at not less than 200,000, which figure is now regarded as excessive."

Prior to the war years and his Presidency, it is difficult to find material bearing on Abraham Lincoln and his association with Jewish citizens. This should not be surprising—outside of Chicago there were not many representative Jews in Illinois, save here and there a successful merchant. Paul M. Angle, in his fine volume on Springfield, Illinois, entitled *Here I Have Lived*, says in a letter to the writer: "You found no mention of Jews in *Here I Have Lived* because there were almost none in Springfield while Lincoln lived there. I never found anything to indicate that Lincoln had any relations with the few Jews whom he might have known in his home town."

The late Emmanuel Hertz, who looked upon Lincoln with something akin to idolatry, and published many books on his favorite theme, confesses his inability to turn up anything of importance relating to Lincoln and the Jews prior to his Presidency, with a single exception, and that, a letter written by Lincoln to a prominent Jewish citizen of Quincy, Illinois. This letter which Hertz reprints in the preface to his *Abraham Lincoln: The Tribute of the Synagogue*, appeared originally in the *Complete Works of Abraham Lincoln* by Nicolay and Hay (Volume VI, pages 41 and 46). Since some readers of this chapter may not have access either to the Nicolay-Hay volume, or to Mr. Hertz' book, not to mention the Markens monograph which is out of print, I include the letter here. It is dated July 21, 1860, and marked "Confidential."

Hon. A. Jonas,
MY DEAR SIR:
Yours of the 2nd is received. I suppose as good or even better men than I may have been in American or Know-Nothing Lodges, but in

point of fact I have never been in one in Quincy or elsewhere. I was never in Quincy but one day and two nights while Know-Nothing lodges were in existence and you were with me that day and both those nights. I have never been there before in my life and never afterwards, till the joint debate with Douglas in 1858. It was in 1854 when I spoke in some hall there, and after the speaking, you with others took me to an oyster saloon, passed an hour there, and you walked with me to, and parted with me at Quincy House quite late at night. I left by stage for Naples before daylight in the morning, having come in by the same route after dark the evening previous to the speaking, where I found you waiting at the Quincy House to meet me. A few days after I was there, Richardson as I understand, started this same story about my having been in a Know-Nothing lodge. When I heard this charge, as I did soon after, I taxed my recollection for some incident which could have suggested it; and I remember that on my parting with you the last night I went to the office of the hotel to take my stage passage for the morning and was told that no stage office for that line was kept there, and that I must see the driver before retiring, to insure his calling for me in the morning; and a servant was sent for me to find the driver, who, after taking me a square or two stopped me, and stepped perhaps a dozen steps farther, and in my hearing called to someone, who answered him apparently from the upper part of a building, and promised to call with the stage for me at the Quincy House. I returned and went to bed, and before day the stage called and took me. This is all. That I was never in a Know-Nothing lodge in Quincy I should expect could be easily proved by respectable men who were always in the lodges and never saw me there. An affidavit of one or two such should put the matter at rest. And now a word of caution. Our adversaries think they can gain a point if they force me openly to deny the charge, by which some degree of offence would be given to the "Americans." For this reason it must not publicly appear that I am paying any attention to the charge.

Yours truly,
A. LINCOLN.

Some inferences are plain from this letter, and one is that Mr. Lincoln and Mr. Jones were friends, and that he was a political supporter of Lincoln. Incidentally, it reveals the political canniness of the Springfield lawyer. And the letter puts Mr. Lincoln on record again as to his opposition to the Know-Nothings, if in truth that were necessary, assuming his letter to Joshua Speed written August 24, 1855, had been made public. But we should like to know more about the writer of this letter, and Dr. Markens supplies the information which follows:

"Abraham Jonas, who was born in Exeter, England, came to Cincinnati in 1819, moved to Williamston, Kentucky, where he married and served in the legislature, settled in Illinois in 1838, and was elected to the legislature there in 1842, and became the first Grand Master of Masons of that state in 1839. Jonas was at the Illinois State Convention held at Bloomington May 29, 1856, and was a Presidential elector on the Fremont ticket." Dr. Markens finds good reasons to believe that the friendship of Lincoln and Jonas was personal as well as political, and there is none to dispute the claim.

II

Upon Mr. Lincoln's election to the Presidency the Jews come more prominently into the records of his administration. For instance, a young English Jew, Dr. Isachar Zacharie became Mr. Lincoln's chiropodist, for whom the President wrote this testimonial: "Dr. Zacharie has operated on my feet with great success and considerable addition to my comfort." This Jewish doctor must have been quite a character, for of him the New York *Herald* said: "Dr. Zacharie trimmed the feet of President Lincoln and his cabinet. He is a wit, a gourmet and eccentric, with a splendid Roman nose, fashionable whiskers, and an eloquent tongue, a dazzling diamond breast-pin, great skill in his profession and an ingratiating address." That Abraham Lincoln bestowed appointments and honors on Jewish citizens beyond any other President of the United States up to his administration is a matter of history.

Lincoln was the first President to appoint a Jewish army chaplain, Dr. Arnold of New York getting the appointment in 1862 after Congress passed special legislation making it possible.

Lincoln was the first President to appoint a Jew as full-fledged minister to a foreign power, the post of minister to Italy having been offered to and refused by Sigismund Kaufmann of New York.

Lincoln appointed a Jew by the name of Einstein United States Consul to Nuremberg, Germany, destined to become the capital of anti-Semitism.

Lincoln countermanded an order promulgated from General Grant's headquarters which excluded all Jews from his department. The revocation came promptly on the President's learning of the order. Even so, there was some excitement over the incident, and an indignation meeting was held by aroused Jews, who demanded General Grant's resignation.

President Lincoln's friendly relationship with Jewish citizens was in harmony with his character and his attitude all along the way. Few politicians have been as free from racial and creedal partisanship as was Mr. Lincoln.

III

Emmanuel Hertz' *Abraham Lincoln: The Tribute of the Synagogue*, to which favorable reference has already been made, is an anthology of sermons and addresses by eminent Jewish leaders, both rabbis and laymen. The book contains seventy-five sermons and addresses, eleven by laymen and sixty-four by rabbis, several of the latter being represented by more than one sermon. Of special importance is the fact that nineteen of these sermons were delivered by rabbis to their congregations from five to thirty days after Mr. Lincoln's death, one on April 15, one April 16, eleven on April 19, one on April 29, three on June 1, one on June 2, and still another on June 10, all of course, in 1865.

The style of the eulogies is solemn and impressive; the tone highly exalted, with praise of Lincoln lavishly bestowed. On the whole there is less emotional restraint exhibited in these noble discourses than appears in most of the noted sermons preached at the same period from Christian pulpits. This is understandable, for these Hebraic panegyrists represented a minority people long oppressed and grievously persecuted, a people of sorrows and acquainted with grief. In Lincoln they saw a modern Moses, who, like him, but glimpsed the Promised Land of peace into which he might not enter.

One of the most noted Jewish leaders during the Presidency of Lincoln, was Rabbi Sabato Morais, founder and first president of the Jewish Theological Seminary of America. For many years he was the rabbi of Congregation Mikveh Israel of Philadelphia. On the day set apart by Presidential proclamation, this rabbi's prayer for the casualties of both armies attracted wide and favorable comment. Under date of May 13, 1862, Mr. Lincoln addressed a letter to A. Hart, president of the Philadelphia congregation, which read as follows:

Permit me to acknowledge the receipt of your communication of April 23rd containing a copy of a prayer recently delivered at your synagogue, and to thank you heartily for your expressions of kindness and confidence.

I have the honor to be
                    Your obedient servant,
                                        A. LINCOLN.

Only recently this letter came to light, and its discovery makes all the more interesting Rabbi Morais' prayer, which follows:

Author of all good! We implore thy almighty protection on behalf of the American republic of the north. Let thine eyes, which never slumber, be open upon her, that she may not be erased from among the family of nations. Be with her in this struggle for life, that she may survive it, and wax greater and happier.

Speak to the hearts of her disaffected children, and let them again throb with undying affection. Let both the weapon of aggression and that of defense be buried into the bottomless ocean, and cast thou with it the spirit of acrimony that has sharpened its edge.

Direct the hands into which the temporal welfare of this people is entrusted. Sustain them that their strength may never flag. Bless the president of the United States; bless him for his sterling honesty. Bless him for his firmness and moderation.

Rekindle with joy his domestic hearth; pour on him the balm of divine consolation. Grant that the issues of his momentous obligations be a united and prosperous country.

Grant that the end of his career be the maintenance of this government, unimpaired and unsullied as bequeathed by our illustrious ancestors. So may it be. Amen.

On Wednesday, April 19, 1865, five days after the assassination, Rabbi Morais delivered an address "On the Death of Abraham Lincoln." He took for his text Joel 2:17, "Let the priests, the ministers of the Lord, weep between the porch and the altar, and let them say, 'O Eternal God! have mercy upon Thy people.'" Then followed a singularly impressive discourse, warm and tender, from which this passage is taken:

Brethren! If the pulsations of my heart could assume human speech, they would best picture my mental agony upon that never-to-be-forgotten Sabbath. I had never concealed before my love for him who was chosen from among the lowly as a ruler over a great people. Yes, I loved every action, every word of that godly man. I loved him for his patriarchal simplicity; I loved him for his incorruptible character; I loved him for his all-comprehensive ideas, for his generous impulses, his forbearing disposition, his tender compassion for all the oppressed. The ideal of Truth imprinted by nature upon my soul, seemed at length realized in that man of homely mien, but of lofty mind. Alas! that many knew not his worth, and misapprehended his deeds! They called him ambitious; but his ambition was to redeem a pledge he had solemnly taken. They imputed to him a despotic sway; but he exercised power to vindicate the law of the living God. They could not see that beneath the crust of apparent dross lay whatsoever is inestimable and precious. But he who grappled with falsehood, and saved America from ignominious death, needs not my defense. He who removed the burden from every shoulder, and wiped off the mark of degradation from human visage, is far above the encomium offered by one so humble as he who speaks on this melancholy occasion. Verily, my friends, did I possess the eloquence of our lamented Everett, I could not extol in adequate terms a man who knew so admirably to temper justice with mercy, and who, while practicing humility in the highest degree, was so scrupulously chary of the national honor . . .

. . . If his paternal voice could reach us from the seat of beatitude, it would exhort us to suffer further privations, to endure hardships, to bear even a temporary defeat, but never to pause until the flag of one reunited people shall wave from Maine to California, from the St. Lawrence to the Gulf of Mexico; for in that event not only our happiness and that of our children is involved, but the cause of human liberty is deeply concerned. If our great Abraham could address us now, he would also beseech us to curb the noble wrath which his murder has aroused within us, lest it may be visited upon the guiltless and the penitent. He would, in his merciful nature, entreat that we prefer magnanimity to severity, forgiveness to vengeance. He would likewise heal our lacerated hearts by the assurance that his mission upon earth was fulfilled, on the day that the supremacy of the Constitution was reasserted, and unspotted hands planted again over the ruins of Fort Sumter the banner which is the symbol of independence and freedom, of justice and humanity. Oh, may his kindly words ever re-echo in our hearts, and incite us to godliness and truth.

On the same day, April 19th, in Temple Emanu-El, New York City, Rabbi Samuel Adler posed a question which has not yet been answered. He thus spoke:

No one knows whether to call Abraham Lincoln, second to Washington or the first? Like Washington he was the defender of freedom and of liberty, both of which attributes he brought about unblemished. His character, determination, energy, and perseverance cause us to call him Father Abraham. Even as God said to Abraham, the patriarch, that he was to be the father of many people, so did God select Abraham Lincoln to be the protector and father of a great people. He was the great sprout which sheltered and protected this Great Nation. He stood firm and did not flinch. Great in spirit, in character, in everything, he resisted every temptation to turn him from the right path. As Moses was meek so was Lincoln. Both lived lowly in spirit, both were respected, loved, and adored, and both died endowed with the same qualities. Abraham Lincoln has not fallen. He is lost to us but he is as Light and an angel with his Father and remains with us in memory and adoration and will so remain for ever.

IV

Tributes to Lincoln still come from the synagogues. The eminent spiritual leaders of congregations both Orthodox and Reformed continue to pay homage to the Moses of the nineteenth century. The great names of Rabbis Magnes, Hirsch, Krass, Harrison, Freehof, Philipson, Enelow, Feldman, Silver, Stephen S. Wise—these and many others are on the shining lists. Rabbi Emil G. Hirsch of Chicago was an enthusiastic admirer of Lincoln, and every anniversary of his hero's birth this famous Jewish leader spoke at length and eloquently. On February 12th, 1909, his subject at the Lincoln centenary celebration at Chicago was "The Great Commoner." In the course of the address Rabbi Hirsch said:

> When he fell, the world wept. They that but yesterday had carried the musket for the defense of what they believed to be their rights, the men who wore the battle-tattered gray, felt that in him they lost their truest friend. Monarchs shed a tear at his bier. The noblest of rulers had ascended to glory. They knew none to the purple born who bore escutcheon more lustrous than was his, the great commoner's.
>
> But we at this hour must not forget that memory spells also monition. How do we measure up against him? He laid tribute on the graves of those that died that the government of the people, for the people, and by the people might not perish. No enemy from without, indeed, is threatening the permanence of our institutions, the independence of our State, the prosperity of our people. We have been garnering the harvest of the day of Appomattox. Ours is now a world empire. But is ours, for all this, a government of the people? Is it not a government

of politicians, for politicians? Serious question this, inviting searching of the heart. Has increase in wealth tended to undemocratize our manners, our ambitions? Has it obscured our ideals, placed near the altar new, strange deities wrought of gold? Are these the Gods that have led us forth out of Egypt, out of the crucible of trial and distress? Has there been profounder reverence for law among us, the heirs of the men that were giants in those gigantic days?

Great men are mountain peaks. As we look up towards the peak named the Martyr-Saviour-President, shall the lifted finger, tipped with the gold of glorious sunshine, not be for us sign and symbol that our way shall lead upwards? The mountain range of which he is the highest point embraces many crests. Grant, Seward, Stanton, Sherman, Sheridan, Logan, Schurz, Sumner, Morton, Yates, Curtis, and a host of other names tell their significance. Yet high as they are, their height is worthily crowned and completed in the one that stands out above all in superb majesty—Abraham Lincoln.

Is it surprising that these Jewish religious teachers saw a Messianic mission in Abraham Lincoln, and that this thought appears again and again in these sermonic tributes? Who would answer in the negative? Not many! Thus Rabbi J. Leonard Levy preaching to the Congregation Rodeph Shalom, Pittsburgh, Pennsylvania, April 16, 1905, said: "He [Lincoln] was America's suffering Messiah. Despised and rejected of men originally, he became the Prophet of the Union. Upon him lay the burden of the people. He was oppressed for the nation; he was destroyed, the victim of the nation's passion."

And on February 7, 1909, before the same congregation, Rabbi Levy likened Lincoln to the Christian's Savior. He said:

Like a Jesus, he was born in a manger. There were no angels to announce his birth, but with his coming there was the assurance of peace on earth and good-will toward men, as well as glory to God in the highest. He was born in poverty, and of him the doubting Nathaniels said: "Can there be any good thing come out of Kentucky?" . . . The plain people loved him. They heard him gladly . . . They accepted him as leader . . . They however placed upon him the crown of thorns . . . He passed through the Gethsemane of trial. He prayed "O that this bitter cup might pass away, but if it be thy will, O Father, thy will be done." He met his end on Calvary, crucified as the truly great have often been. Buried, he rose again, and he has since become a spirit immortal.

And Rabbi Bernard Revel, on February 12, 1909, at a centenary celebration of Lincoln's birth, held in New York City, said: "Moreover in Lincoln himself were fused all the essentials of Judaism. If he can justly be called the first typical American, he can more justly be said to represent the summation of the noblest qualities of Judaism."

And Rabbi Isaac M. Wise as far back as April 19, 1865, in a memorial address delivered in Lodge Street Temple, Cincinnati, Ohio, made this remarkable statement: "Brethren, the lamented Abraham Lincoln believed himself to be bone from our bone and flesh from our flesh. He supposed himself to be a descendent of Hebrew parentage. He said so in my presence. And indeed he preserved numerous features of the Hebrew race, both in countenance and character."

Commenting on this statement, the careful historian, Dr. Isaac Markens, says: "As a matter of fact Lincoln's knowledge of his ancestry was vague—so much so that his statement to Dr. Wise must be accepted as nothing more than a bit of pleasantry." Robert T. Lincoln states in reply to an inquiry of the writer that he had "never before heard that his father supposed he had any Jewish ancestry."

In reading these eloquent tributes of synagogue and temple it is not easy to select the one excerpt that should worthily illustrate the fine quality of all of them, but after some reflection the choice is a paragraph from the address of Rabbi Nathan Krass, delivered at the Buffalo Ad Club, Buffalo, New York, February 12, 1914. Perhaps my personal acquaintance and vast admiration for Dr. Krass has had something to do with this selection, but certainly not altogether so,

PHINEAS D. GURLEY

MATTHEW SIMPSON

PETER CARTWRIGHT

HENRY WARD BEECHER

for the intrinsic strength and beauty of the rabbi's tribute is notably great:

I was asked to draw some lessons from the life of Lincoln for our own generation. Well, one such lesson is this. It is not an essential of greatness to hold one's self aloof from one's fellowmen. Such is the method of near-greatness. The greater the man, the more will he love and labor for and live with his fellowmen. The old biblical verses are still true—the first in the old, the second in the new testaments. "And the oldest shall serve the youngest, the more powerful the weaker." "The greatest among you shall serve the least." This lesson was supremely illustrated in the personality of Lincoln and that is one of many legacies he has left us in our great democracy. He left one more, which I shall mention. It was said that Lincoln was not a churchman. Well, what of it? I can name some others that were not in the technical sense churchmen. And I do this not by way of criticism of the church, but reverently. For there have been great exceptions in the religious world who stood outside the organized church not because they were irreligious, but because they were temperamentally more comfortable outside of the church. Moses was no churchman. Yet, he was profoundly religious. The prophets were not churchmen. Yet, they are the greatest group of religious souls the world has ever seen or heard. Jesus was no churchman. Yet, in the hearts of all these characters, there was that deep, that powerful, that vitalizing sense of spirituality, that absolute feeling of direct communion with God that transcends all externalities.

In this sense, Abraham Lincoln was an intensely religious soul. He believed, and that is his other legacy to us, that real religion is spirituality in action, that divine service is service to humanity, and we are learning that lesson as we never learned it before.

You are familiar with Churchill's novel, *The Inside of the Cup*. And you recall the description of the church pillars. In Buffalo, as in New York, you will find many church pillars. Pillars are made of stone, and often the human pillars of churches are stony-hearted who lend grace and social status, but no soul and service. They are not religious men. They are not like Lincoln, whose creed was not an oppressive chain around his neck, a contracting gyve around his heart, but whose religion was an open sesame to humanity. And how he loved humanity.

"God surely loved the common people, he made so many of them" was one of his familiar sayings. And the religion of democracy, learning its lesson and gaining its inspiration from Lincoln, is none other than the religion without hate and prejudice, that will not cause a tear to flow, but will brush it off the cheek of sorrow and suffering and pain. You may call this religion Judaism. You may name it Christianity. It matters not. Lincoln was so big that every creed claims him. In his soul, there burned the divine essentials that make all religions glow. We would honor Lincoln's memory? Let us emulate him in his idealism. It warmed the souls of millions. We would twine a literary laurel wreath about his name? Remember that in his heart there blossomed the finest flowers that diffused their sweet aroma across a continent and caused stifling, stumbling humanity to inhale a whiff of that which strengthens and uplifts.

With a single verbal alteration, let my final word be a paragraph from Lincoln's eulogy of Washington. "On that name no eulogy is expected. It cannot be. To add brightness to the sun, or glory to the name of Lincoln is alike impossible. Let none attempt it. In solemn awe pronounce the name and in its naked, deathless splendor leave it shining on!"

Thus we have heard from the rabbis of synagogue and temple in their praise of Abraham Lincoln.[1] For the last word, we turn to a poet of the synagogue, Leon Huhuer, who wrote:

[1] There is a string of episodes and events which curiously tie together Jewish affairs and personalities with Abraham Lincoln: The last photograph of Lincoln, taken on the Sunday before his assassination, was made in the Washington studio of Adolphus Solomons, later president of B'nai B'rith, showing the President sharpening a pencil for his son . . . The first public utterances in connection with the death of Lincoln were heard in the synagogues because Lincoln died on a Saturday . . . Dr. C. H. Lieberman, Washington Jewish physician, was one of nine medical men at Lincoln's deathbed, and his portrait is among the forty-seven persons in the famous painting, "The Last Hours of Lincoln" . . . The Hashkabah, the Sephardic funeral rite, was recited in a Jewish house of worship for any other than professing the Jewish religion for the first time in Shearith Israel Synagogue, New York, during a Lincoln memorial service . . . The "Hebrew citizens" of Alton, Illinois, were the first contributors to the fund raised to erect a Lincoln monument at Springfield, Illinois . . . Edward Rosewater, later founder and editor of the Omaha *Bee* transmitted to the world from the telegraph office of the War Department, Lincoln's Emancipation Proclamation . . . The Lincoln

Our Lincoln came not from the learned few,
But from the struggling humble multitude,
Whose cares he shared and whose distress he knew;
Equipped he came with love and fortitude,
That he might cut the canker out, and then
With gentle hand heal up the wound again.

penny, the first coin bearing the head of a President, which was issued on August 2, 1909, was designed by a Jewish artist, Victor D. Brenner, whose initials "VDB" appeared on the first twenty-eight million of these coins.

Chapter XI

The Tribute of the Churches

Preachers' lips were touched with fire.

* *

THE bullet that struck down Abraham Lincoln inspired a deluge of funereal oratory seldom, if ever, equalled at any other place or time. It is reasonable to believe that no less than ten thousand memorial sermons were preached in the United States, Canada, and Great Britain during that season of sorrow. Every denomination was represented, not excepting the Roman Catholic clergy, seldom given to fulsome sermons over the dead. From city cathedral to the humblest rural meetinghouse a sermonic tidal wave swept the nation.

The tragic manner of President's Lincoln's death helps to account for the unprecedented tributes in synagogue and church but does not wholly explain it. Presidents Garfield and McKinley were also victims of assassins' bullets, but nothing like the notice the pulpits took of Lincoln's passing followed the death of these two Presidents, though they too were beloved by millions.

The kindly nature of Lincoln, his almost sublime patience, vast gentleness, quality of mercy and forgiveness, had much to do with the grief that submerged the nation and much of the world that "wild spring of pain." Then too, there was something in Lincoln's physical structure which set him apart from other men. In death as in life he was not easy to forget—the huge loose-jointed body; the heavily

furrowed face; the sad, deep-set eyes; the humorous mouth—all combined to make him "the quaint great figure that men love," as Vachel
Lindsay would have it.

Then again the awful blow was struck at an hour calculated to
shock the nation as at no other time. A dreadful internecine war
had just ended, the wounds of which were still raw and bleeding.
The half a million men, North and South, who were dead, had
widowed and orphaned thousands of families. Emotions were easily
stirred, nerves were taut, the people as sheep without a shepherd.
At such a time they naturally turned to the churches, the solace of
religion, and their spiritual leaders for consolation, as well as to hear
them extol the virtues of the fallen Chieftain.

I

No other Lincoln author to my knowledge made so dramatic a
literary use of the sermons preached following President Lincoln's
assassination as did Lloyd Lewis in his well-written book *Myths After
Lincoln*, published in 1929. In this work Mr. Lewis devotes three
chapters to what the preachers said from their pulpits during those
grief-drenched days. The titles of his chapters are illuminating,
namely, "Black Easter," "They Knew What God Wanted," and
"The Dying God." This competent writer handled his material with
the practiced skill of an experienced craftsman, and the result, while
enlightening, is not always edifying. That there is extravagance of
expression in some of the sermons, and questionable taste in a few,
is true, but it is doubtful if the sorrowing multitudes which filled the
churches were conscious of any flaws in the sermons to which they
gave rapt and sympathetic hearing, for the sentiments and emotions
of the preachers mirrored quite faithfully the tortured minds and
aching hearts of the grief-scourged nation. Seldom was it truer, "like
people, like priest."

This present writer comes naturally to a review of these sermons
of fellow clergymen preached in painful circumstances and amidst

fear and anxiety with no small commiseration and a fellow-feeling of understanding and sympathy. He feels much as a fellow surgeon who watches a difficult and delicate operation, or as a lawyer might feel as he observes a brother barrister in the conduct of a famous and exacting lawsuit with much at stake.

On the whole the tribute of the Christian pulpit stands up well, as does also that of the synagogue. If there are mountains and valleys in the sermonic topography, so likewise there is an elevated and spacious plateau of sustained strength and excellence.

II

The emotions of the preachers as they came up to such an Easter Sunday as they had never before known, is aptly voiced by the Rev. Cyrus A. Bartol, of Boston, as he stood up to preach that Easter Sunday in 1865. He said:

> I am unable to give and you perhaps indisposed to receive any regular preaching today. If I can but tell you what is in the air: if I can voice your feeling and my own, still more the spirit of God which is ready to be voiced by human lips, the real end of our meeting will, however informally, be reached. I lay aside therefore my written discourse, though it be ecclesiastically a festival this morning. No Romish rubric has a right to prescribe our theme. I take no text save from the Bible of providence, the great book of events. God's finger is still writing in burning words every hour. I accept his subject and defer my own.

Likewise, the Rev. John E. Todd at Pittsfield, Massachusetts, exhibited the stress under which he and his fellow preachers spoke that solemn Easter, as he declared:

> The first emotion experienced by everyone upon being informed of this terrible event was one of unmitigated horror, and it is a feeling from which we have not yet recovered. There were various things fitted to intensify it. We had not yet recovered from the ecstasies of delight occasioned by victories unprecedented in modern warfare, and which

gave promise of speedy peace. The terrible tidings found us on the heights of exultation, and the fall in our feelings, and the shock, were proportionately tremendous.

The preacher continues in vivid sentences:

The tidings were too terrible to be comprehended or credited at once: the President foully assassinated in the very presence of the people, with deliberate forethought: the Secretary of State stabbed while lying on a sickbed, and his attendants killed and wounded. Other important officers of government—the Secretary of War, the Lieutenant General of the United States Army—escaped only, without doubt, in consequence of unexpected detention from the President's side. Such was the dreadful story. It was ticked off first at midnight to a few blanched faces, and was rejected. It came again with stronger authority. It stared out in grim and terrible lines from the morning papers, making the brain of the reader to reel, and the heart to grow sick. It was told in husky and frightened tones by one to another, and with voices choked with tears. It leaped from face to face, pale and livid, as we never saw the faces of the people before. It began to fringe the flags, and to darken the streets which were but recently so gay. It began to create gloom, and a hush and loneliness in business haunts, which but a few days since were filled with crowds and processions, and cheers and music. It began to wail from steeple to steeple. It broke at last from the cannon's mouth in solemn thunder. And at length, we begin to realize today, that our president is no more.

This is graphic, dramatic, moving descriptive eloquence. What the Rev. John E. Todd felt that day, those who heard him also felt. But these preachers did not stop with vivid word pictures. They paid tribute to the mighty dead, and comforted their weeping congregations.

The Rev. George H. Hepworth, D.D., also of Boston, in an analysis of Mr. Lincoln's character was ingenious even when voicing a mild criticism of what might seem to be certain deficiencies in the late President:

If a stranger were to offer his criticism upon Mr. Lincoln, I think the first characteristic of which he would speak would be the extreme and charming simplicity of the man. This is so marked a peculiarity, that no one can have failed to notice it. It is to be observed, not only in his daily talk, and in his always courteous bearing, but also in his public addresses, and in those documents, some of which are to become a part of our national literature. He is the most truly Republican President we have ever had. Occupying a position as important and as influential as that of the Emperor of France, he carried to the White House the rigid simplicity of his Illinois home; and in his endeavor to do the work—the arduous work of the hour—he forgot to put on any of the trappings or pomp of royalty. So noticeable was this peculiarity, that many regretted what we called a certain want of refinement. We would have had him keep in remembrance that he was President of the United States; but he could never ignore the fact that he was simply Abraham Lincoln. To say what he meant, was his ambition; and to mean what he said, was a matter of honor. Perhaps he did not always indulge in court language; perhaps he was not as graceful as some lesser men have been; but he always acted the wise, the prudent, and manly part . . . Grace of bearing is a good thing; but unswerving integrity is sublime, even when it is awkward.

This is very good, and there is more like it in this, one of the best of the numerous sermons preached that April "when lilacs last in the dooryard bloomed."

III

That orator-preacher of Ciceronian eloquence, the Rev. Richard S. Storrs, Jr., D.D., of Brooklyn, New York, on June 1, 1865, at the request of the War Fund Committee, delivered a eulogy which ranks with Beecher's in grand passages. Only two of his magnificent paragraphs are presented here, but they will suffice to reveal the splendor of his rhetoric:

At his [Lincoln's] entrance on his office he found the leaders of the largest, fiercest, and most confident rebellion known to history, apparently in all things superior to himself—in capacity, in culture, in political experience, in control over men, in general weight with the country itself. And when he was assassinated, he left them so utterly overthrown and discomfited that they fled over seas, or hid themselves in women's clothes. A power it had taken thirty years to mature, a power that put everything into the contest—money, men, harbors, homes, churches, cities, states themselves,—and they fought with a fury never surpassed, he not only crushed but extinguished in four years. A court that had been the chief bulwark of Slavery, he so re-organized as to make it a citadel of liberty and light for all time to come. He found a race enmeshed in a bondage which had lasted already two hundred years, and had been only compacted and confirmed by invention and commerce, by arts, legislations, by social usage, by ethnic theories, and even by what was called religion; he pretended to no special fondness for the race; he refused to make war on its own behalf; but he took it up cheerfully in the sweep of his plans, and left it a race of free workers and soldiers . . .

The Heavens are his home. But the earth and the records will take care of his fame, for of all whom he meets and dwells with there, no one has held a higher trust; no one been more loyal to it; no one has left a work behind more grand and vast. And so long as the Government which he reestablished shall continue to endure; so long as the Country which he made again the home of one nation shall hold that nation within its compass, and shall continue to attract to its bosom the liberty-loving from every land; so long as the people which he emancipated shall make the palmetto and the orange tree quiver with the hymns of its jubilee; so long as the race which he has set forward shall continue to advance, through brightening paths, to the Future that waits for its swift steps,—a fame as familiar as any among men, a character as distinguished, and an influence as wide, will be the fame, the character, and the influence, of him who came four years ago an unknown man from his home in the West, but who has now written in letters of light, on pages as grand and as splendid as any in the history of the world the illustrious name of Abraham Lincoln.

Let us hear a voice from across the sea, that of the Rev. Newman Hall, who preached in Surrey Chapel, London, on Sunday, May 14, 1865, a sermon on "The Assassination of Abraham Lincoln." A less powerful and more plaintive voice than that of the Rev. Dr. Storrs, it still deserves to be heard:

There has been no death in our own day more remarkable, none which will have a more prominent place in all future history, than the assassination of President Lincoln. If it was appropriate that every pulpit in our land should make allusion to the death of our lamented Prince Consort, if the omission would have argued a culpable disloyalty,—is it not right, that in all the churches of America, sermons have been delivered with special reference to the death of the President? If we were bereaved as a nation, should we not feel grateful for the sympathy of Americans if they also, in public worship alluded to our loss? So also it is fitting, that throughout our country such sympathy in public worship has been and still is manifested, especially when we consider the unparalleled atrocity of the deed which has deprived them of their Chief Magistrate, and the peculiar crisis of affairs at which he has been taken from them.

There is cause for lamentation. A good and a great man has fallen by the hand of an assassin, who thought that in striking down the nation's head, he was striking down the nation itself. The universal grief in America shows how he was honored and beloved. Twice chosen by the free voice of millions of his fellow-citizens to rule over them in the most momentous crisis of their history; twice chosen to steer the vessel of the State amid waves that threatened to overwhelm it; exposed to their keen scrutiny in all his public and private acts,—he has won their universal homage and affection. Beneath an exterior unlike that which is generally found in courts, and which gave occasion to vulgar satirists to utter their rude jests, there beat a heart to which courts have been too much strangers. In President Lincoln there was a combination of honesty, sagacity, magnanimity, and gentleness such as few rulers have ever manifested. He was faithful to the trust imposed on him. He was firm to the purpose he had maturely formed. He was true to the nation whose integrity he was sworn to maintain. He was true to those principles of freedom he had always professed and loved. He would not allow his benevolent impulses to lead him away from what he considered his duty to the State which he had engaged to govern according to law. Neither would he allow his official position to deaden and keep in abeyance those impulses. The fear of misrepresentation, the charge of inconsistency, did not cause him to waver in the course he had marked out for himself. He faithfully administered those laws; but as fast as circumstances gave him the opportunity constitutionally to modify those laws in the interest of emancipation, such opportunity was promptly embraced. Those who have not studied the peculiar Constitution of the United States cannot appreciate the difficulty of a President urged on one side by a powerful party and his oath to observe the laws; and urged on the other side by another powerful party and his benevolent sentiments to abolish slavery. History will honor him for having accomplished both tasks.

On June 1, 1865, the day appointed by the President as one of "humiliation and prayer," the Rev. Phineas Gurley preached a sermon on "The Voice of the Rod," and took for text Micah 6:9: "Hear ye the rod, and who hath appointed it." Dr. Gurley divided his sermon into five divisions, thus:

1. The Rod of Chastening Which We Feel Today Teaches Us to Acknowledge and Adore the Sovereignty of God.

2. The Rod of Chastening Which We Feel Today Teaches Us the Duty of Depending upon God with an Exclusive and an Abiding Confidence.

3. Again, the Rod of Chastening Which We Feel Today Suggests to Us That When a Great Mission Is To Be Accomplished for God and Humanity, It Is Sometimes Necessary That He Who Accomplishes It Should Also Seal It with His Blood.

4. Again the Chastening Rod Which We Feel Today Suggests to Us What Is the Real Tendency, and What Are the Diabolical Capabilities and Achievements of That Combined Spirit of Treason and Slavery with Which We Have Been Contending for the Last Four Years.

5. Finally, the Rod of Chastening Which We Feel Today Suggests a Lesson Touching the Character and Influence of the Theatre, Which We Should Note and Remember.

Under this last heading the pastor and friend of Abraham Lincoln said:

It will always be a matter of deep regret to thousands that our lamented President fell in the theatre; that the dastardly assassin found him, shot him there. Multitudes of his best friends—I mean his Christian friends—would have preferred that he should have fallen in almost any other place. Had he been murdered in his bed, or in his office, or on the street, or on the steps of the Capitol, the tidings of his death would not have struck the Christian heart of the country quite so painfully; for the feelings of the heart is that the theatre is one of the last places to which a good man should go, and among the very last in which his friends would wish him to die. Little or nothing has been said upon this subject in the pulpit or by the religious press; but it is one of the cases in which silence is more expressive than words, and, therefore, I shall say no more.

This statement grates on our ears today and seems incredibly narrow, but it represented probably ninety per cent of Protestant church people of that period, both members of the congregations and their ministers. This is the only occasion on record where Dr. Gurley referred to Lincoln's being in a theater when the assassin struck him down, and deploring the place where he fell. He had other opportunities to do so, notably at the funeral services in the White House where Dr. Gurley preached the sermon. Thus his reference in this sermon preached six weeks after the death of the President reveals both the considerateness of the man and the stout convictions he held, and his readiness to defend them at what he felt to be a suitable time.

Nor was the Catholic pulpit silent as a mighty chorus of tributes rose from Protestant and Jewish pulpits. In St. Louis on April 19, 1865, in the Church of the Holy Ghost, the Rev. Hugo Krebs preached an eloquent Easter sermon and drew a parallel between the deaths of Christ and Lincoln on Good Friday. Some paragraphs translated from the German by a woman who was present are here appended:

Now then, my friends, who stand lamenting by the grave of Abraham Lincoln, shall no Easter morning follow our political Good Friday;

shall the words: *Why seek ye the living by the dead?* have been spoken in vain for us?

Abraham Lincoln, born in Bourbon County,[1] Kentucky, the man, who, after a youth passed without cultivation, after long and arduous struggles, after earnest labor with ax and pen, with hand and head, attained the highest honors, which our land can bestow upon a citizen. The man, who lived long in Springfield, Illinois, and will also rest there; the man, who so calmly and firmly steered our Ship of State; that man is certainly dead, murdered by a ruthless hand, still I say in the same moment with fullest conviction: *He lives! Why seek ye the living by the dead?*

Without doubt, my friends, the tall, meager, friendly man, called *Abraham Lincoln*, whom anyone could see as he rode or walked through the streets of the Capital, this visible, corporeal President of the United States of America—is dead—nevertheless, I say: *He lives! Why seek ye the living by the dead?*

That, which we see and touch, is not the real, the abiding, the essential part of man; that is the perishable, the mortal part, the semblance; the immortal part of man, this is his spirit, his principles, his thoughts.

Men die, but their principles die not; men die, but their thoughts live forever. The spirit, which animated them is victorious over death, and lives forth in the race of men. Although we see death daily, and experience his terrors in our immediate presence, still we believe in life; then the world transfigures itself to a revelation of the spirit, and man to a temple of God.

The two cherished ideas of the beloved dead were: *Liberty and Love*. Liberty for all without distinction of color or birth, a union of all in love, a firm, lasting union of all from the North to the South, from the Atlantic to the Pacific. These are Christian thoughts, this is true Christianity, this is eternal truth.

Abraham Lincoln lives, and will fill this continent with his spirit, and with his *eternal principles* of truth will conquer the world. Freedom and equality to all, love of all to all!

Men die daily, but the TRUTH RISES DAILY FROM THE GRAVE, and will gradually obtain universal dominion.

However enemies rave, truth, liberty and love will conquer, and so true as God is all powerful his Kingdom will come; and his creative

[1] An error; should be Hardin County.

word: "LET THERE BE LIGHT," will—in a political and social sense—first be fulfilled in our land.

Before my mind's eye stands the future and I see—although it may be a dream, still it is a prophetic dream—the glorious starry banner floating from the Polar Sea to the shores of Mexico, waving over these free United States of all North America; and in the clouds I see the form of our beloved martyr whom we mourn today, standing by the side of his Redeemer, and from the lips of both float down the words upon our land:

"Peace be with you!

"Amen!"

IV

The tributes of the pulpits to the memory of Abraham Lincoln continue unabated and seem in truth to gather momentum with the flight of the years. Every anniversary of the Emancipator's birth, memorial sermons are announced and delivered by the thousands. One has but to read the church page in his newspaper to be reminded how Lincoln conscious is the American pulpit. It is not unreasonable to put the number of sermons and addresses given annually by Christian preachers and Jewish rabbis at five to ten thousand, and the estimate is likely to prove conservative. Practically one minister and rabbi out of three has prepared at least one sermon or address on Lincoln; some of them half a dozen.

In 1909, the centenary of Lincoln's birth, the output of sermons and addresses by clergymen of all faiths, but principally Protestant, was prodigious. In 1910, Nathan William MacChesney edited and published a volume entitled *Abraham Lincoln, The Tribute of A Century.* Conspicuous in the collections are addresses by these clergymen: Rev. A. J. Carey and Rev. J. W. E. Bowen, [Negroes], Rabbi Emil G. Hersch, Rev. Charles J. Little, D.D, Rev. Lyman Abbott, D.D., Rev. Jenkin Lloyd Jones, D.D., Rev. Dr. Henry Van Dyke, and Bishop William F. McDowell, D.D.

Dr. Newell Dwight Hillis, who followed second in succession of Henry Ward Beecher at Plymouth Church, Brooklyn, preached on several memorable occasions with Abraham Lincoln as his theme. On February 12, 1923, Dr. Hillis delivered a scintillating sermon on "Abraham Lincoln," taking for his text John 1:6: "There was a man sent from God":

> In pathos and tragedy, his story is unequalled in all the history of misfortune touched with grandeur and sorrow mingled with absolute power. Not even the carpenter of Galilee, cradled in a stable, entered life lower than this child opening his eyes in a cheerless log cabin. History holds the story of none who passed from a cradle to a throne so glorious. Looking upon his marred face, Lincoln seems the saddest, sweetest, bravest, gentlest, most picturesque and pathetic figure in human history. . . Looking back, his little cabin shames our ceiled houses. His three or four books rebuke our listlessness midst vast libraries. His six months on a rude school bench rebukes our ignorance after fifteen years in college. His humble poverty dims the lustre of our gold.

The Rev. William A. (Billy) Sunday, picturesque and acrobatic evangelist who swept gustily over the nation in a series of revivals, from 1904 to 1924, or thereabouts, merits a place in this sermonic hall of fame. Sunday climaxed one of his discourses with a dramatization of Lincoln's rise from "lowly earth to the vaulted skies" unique in the history of the American platform or pulpit. It is necessary to get the setting of this remarkable performance in mind.

Picture the big tabernacle with its huge platform on which stood a couple of chairs, a small table, and—the acrobatic Billy Sunday! Imagine the eager thousands who had come together from hundreds of farms and scores of villages and county-seat towns. They expected something to happen, and it surely did, right before their eyes.

In order to dramatize the obscurity, privation, and poverty of the child born in the backwoods of Kentucky, Sunday flung himself flat on the floor of the platform; then . . . slowly raised himself on one elbow to indicate the gangling youth in Indiana reading some treasured volume by the light of a pine-knot fire . . . next he lifted him self abruptly to his knees, thus describing the Salem storekeepe greatening in community esteem and spending his spare hours porin over a volume of Blackstone's Law Commentaries . . . Swiftly Sunda mounted a chair to signify the nation-wide fame that came to him as a result of lawyer Lincoln's debates with Senator Douglas. At thi juncture Billy leaped with a shout of triumph to the top of the table, to represent Lincoln's election to the Presidency; and standin there with shoulders squared and chin outthrust, he recounted in vivid sentences the burden of the terrible war years on the weary man in the White House. To illustrate the assassination in Ford's Theate and the President's passing, Billy drew from an inside pocket of hi coat a huge white handkerchief, and waving it aloft in wide circle gave what someone described as "a Chautauqua salute to God! By this time five thousand persons were on their feet waving hand kerchiefs and singing the "Battle Hymn of the Republic."

It was immense!

It is fitting that the Rev. Joseph Fort Newton, D.D., bring to close this symposium of pulpit eloquence dedicated to the memory o Abraham Lincoln. Following is the closing paragraph from a sermon preached by Dr. Newton in City Temple, London, England, 1918

No man ever had a loftier conception of the sanctity of law, of th sacramental meaning of the state, than Lincoln had. His oath of offic was a vow of consecration. As meditative as Marcus Aurelius, and a blithe as Mark Twain, as simple as Aesop, yet as subtle as an Orienta a calm, grave strong man, formidable and sad, he stood in the Whit House a high priest of Humanity, an awe-struck ministrant in th Temple of God performing the rites of liberty, justice and pity—pre siding over an offering of blood and fire and tears! He was a ma of God, plain, homely, kindly, who knew that humanity is deepl wounded somewhere, and tried to heal it—and of his fame there wi be no end.

So endeth the long lesson! [2]

[2] Other famous American clergymen who preached memorial sermons following resident Lincoln's death were Rev. Phillips Brooks, Philadelphia, Rev. Theodore uyler, Brooklyn, Rev. Stephen Chipman Thrall, New York, Rev. Edward verett Hale, Boston, Rev. James Freeman Clark, Boston, Rev. Horatio Stebbins, ev. A. L. Stone, Rev. Thomas Starr King, all of California, Rev. Henry W. ellows, Brooklyn, Rev. John H. Barrows, Chicago, Rev. Robert Collyer, New ork, Rev. Howard Crosby, New York, Rev. O. B. Frothingham, New York, ev. Philip Schaff, New York.

Chapter XII

The Speech of Lincoln

"A word fitly spoken is like apples of gold in baskets of silver."

✳✳✳✳✳✳✳✳✳✳✳✳✳✳✳✳✳✳✳✳✳✳✳✳✳✳✳✳✳✳✳✳✳✳✳✳

IT MAY SEEM strange to some students of oratory to find Abraham Lincoln ranked among the lords of speech of the English speaking world. He had few if any of the graces which are usually associated with the great orators. He lacked an impressive and musical voice, charm and grace of delivery. As an after-dinner speaker or a finished popular lecturer the tall, lank Illinois lawyer could not qualify. Yet he belongs to the ages, as a master of words.

When compared with his contemporaries of the platform, a surface judgment would place him below their highest level. He could not equal the urbanity, exuberance and gorgeous oratory of an Ingersoll; the poised, brilliant and epigrammatic genius of a Wendell Phillips; the massive, oracular eloquence of a Webster; or the popular, irresistible oratory of a Henry Clay. He was outrivaled in wide range of versatile dramatic power by a Henry Ward Beecher, and the elegant and polished periods of an Everett were not for him. Nevertheless, a half dozen of Lincoln's speeches equal and indeed outshine the finest of these eloquent men of a golden age of oratory.

What American orators are best known to us? The answer is not difficult. Patrick Henry, because of the two memorable speeches which made him "the tongue of the Revolution"; Daniel Webster because of half a dozen speeches, and especially the glorious peroration to his speech in reply to Senator Hayne of South Carolina; and Abraham Lincoln, because of his Gettysburg Address and the Second Inaugural.

Ingersoll is remembered for his sad and lovely tribute at the graveside of his brother; Blaine, because of the beautiful paragraph which crowns his eulogy on James A. Garfield; Conkling, for his scintillating speech nominating Grant for a third term; and Bryan, for his spectacular "Cross of Gold" speech at Chicago in 1896. As for Woodrow Wilson, his war speeches were as potent as bullets; posterity will probably rank his eloquence high. Granting the genius of these orators, it must be conceded that they rank in the public mind far below Henry, Webster and Lincoln.

Henry Clay was a name in the oratorical firmament of his day to conjure with. Who recalls a single speech of Clay's today? Sargeant S. Prentiss of Mississippi was ranked at the top of mighty orators in a mighty age of oratory by Wendell Phillips and Daniel Webster, excellent judges of eloquence. But Prentiss is not even a name to millions. Thomas Corwin and Thomas Marshall, the Breckinridges of Kentucky—these spoke with the "tongues of angels," but their fame is largely local. The fame of Henry and Webster is nation-wide; Lincoln's, world-wide. And it is so, not solely because of his words, but because Abraham Lincoln's words and deeds matched his heroic hour.

I

Mr. Lincoln's noblest oratory was the eloquence of truth, the setting forth simply and convincingly the rightness of certain causes, basic principles of government and policies. Thus, in his Cooper Institute speech, regarded by some as the high-water level of his forensic oratory, the clear analysis of the issues, the clean-cut logic of the reasoning, more than compensated for the lack of grace and the rustic homeliness, which, as he arose and began the speech, grated on the sensibilities of his cultured hearers. It was what he said, rather than the way he said it; yet he said it with power and in places with beauty.

His was also the eloquence of moral earnestness. It rang true and struck home with the ringing note of sincerity. It was honest thinking. There was much at stake. The unity of the nation was involved in a titanic struggle for existence. The faith of the founding fathers was on trial. The familiarity of the speaker with the historic documents—The Declaration of Independence and the Constitution of the United States—over which he had pored and dreamed as a youth, was an asset and he handled their doctrines with a sure grasp. There was no "window dressing," no parading. He was out to make converts, he was preaching for a verdict.

Lincoln's eloquence, certainly his mature public speaking, was free from what is known as playing to the galleries. He was out to awaken the slumbering conscience of a generation complacent and seemingly indifferent to the dangers that threatened the Republic. The time was past for the mere frippery and froth of speech, and "purple patches" were out of place. Skillful as Lincoln was with an apt story, he did not resort to humor in the speeches that give him his fame as an orator. He was engaged in too serious a task, and the time was short. Thus the high seriousness of his platform utterances and state papers.

Most speeches that live in the minds of the people are brief, meaty and memorable because of the content, the occasion, or both. Patrick Henry's "Give Me Liberty or Give Me Death" speech is brief; Ingersoll's address at his brother's grave is briefer still; Woodrow Wilson's speech in the church at Carlisle, England, the city where his mother was born, is less than four hundred words in length. Lincoln's Cooper Union speech is the longest of his most famous utterances; the First Inaugural is fairly long, while the Farewell Address on leaving Springfield and the speech at Gettysburg are very short. The Second Inaugural, in the judgment of this writer the supreme example of Lincolnian eloquence, is only a fourth the length of his First Inaugural. To be able to compress great ideas and far-reaching principles into a few paragraphs is an art that few public speakers have mastered. Jesus of Nazareth was able to do this, although His Sermon on the Mount as reported by St. Matthew occupies three chapters and consists of one hundred and six verses. His parables are marvels of beauty and the incomparable story of the Prodigal Son is told in twenty-two verses.

The art of a public speaker is seen at its strategic best in his opening and closing sentences and paragraphs. Look at Lincoln's. Thus at Springfield, June 16, 1858, following his nomination for United States Senator, he begins with a pertinent sentence: "If we could first know where we are, and whither we are tending, we could better judge what to do and how to do it."

The farewell on leaving Springfield, February 11, 1861—how this sentence fits the mood of the speaker and the people: "No one not in my situation can appreciate my feeling of sadness at this parting."

Gettysburg, November 19, 1863—he plunges at once into the heart of his immortal utterance: "Fourscore and seven years ago, our fathers brought forth on this continent a new nation, conceived in liberty, and dedicated to the proposition that all men are created equal."

The closing sentence of the Cooper Institute speech is notable since it summarized and clinched his points: "Let us have faith that right makes might, and in that faith let us to the end dare to do our duty as we understand it."

The last sentence at Gettysburg[1] is long, periodic, clear as crystal, and truly eloquent and, more, it is prophetic:

[1] Paul L. Blakely in *America* for November 1942 says: "The Gettysburg Address contains only 297 words. Of these 191 are monosyllables and fifty-seven are words of two syllables. Lincoln did not know much about words and their roots, but he knew how to make them serve him."

It is rather for us to be here dedicated to the great task remaining before us—that from these honored dead we take increased devotion to that cause for which they gave the last full measure of devotion— that we here highly resolve that these dead shall not have died in vain —that this nation, under God, shall have a new birth of freedom and that government of the people, by the people, for the people, shall not perish from the earth.

It is doubtful if any other lord of speech ever put as much in a single shining sentence as did Abraham Lincoln in closing his Second Inaugural address. It is not only an example of flawless English, it is likewise suffused with the spirit of the Great Galilean—humility, forgiveness and boundless love. It is Lincoln's finest and noblest utterance:

> With malice toward none, with charity for all, with firmness in the right as God gives us to see the right, let us strive on to finish the work we are in, to bind up the nation's wounds, to care for him who shall have borne the battle, and for his widow and his orphan, to do all which may achieve and cherish a just and a lasting peace among ourselves and with all nations.

II

It has been said that Lincoln's physical presence lacked grace, but it certainly did not lack power and impressiveness. His height, six feet four, gave him platform advantage; there was a majesty and dignity in his appearance that no ungainliness could offset. His towering figure commanded respect and there was a rustic charm about the man who said his life story was told in the lines of Thomas Gray, "The short and simple annals of the poor."

Voice means much to a public speaker. A mellifluous voice is sometimes a handicap and mesmerizes the listener who may love the sound of it above everything else. There have been some great speakers whose voices were not of the first order. Edmund Burke's voice was said to have been harsh, and Talmadge, who had a great following in his day, had a voice described by some as raucous. Even so great a preacher as Phillips Brooks possessed a voice characterized as throaty, and yet how effective he was. Most of those who heard Lincoln speak referred to his voice as high-pitched and penetrating but never as falsetto. On the other hand, we have the testimony of one of his bearers, himself a notable speaker, who thought Lincoln's voice was remarkable. That man was Dr. Moncure D. Conway, who heard the Illinoisan at Cincinnati, Ohio, in 1859. Writing of the event he said, "On the whole Lincoln's appearance was not attractive until one heard his voice, which possessed variety of expression, earnestness and shrewdness in every tone. The charm of his manner was that he had no manner; he was simple, direct, humorous."

The fame of the orator is ephemeral so far as the effect upon his hearers is concerned. The tone of his voice, the flash of his eyes, the expression of his face, these are as evanescent as the scent of a flower or the splendor of a sunset. Nor are these easy to describe. They must be seen and felt in order to be fairly appraised. But the content of the orator's speeches lives on provided they deserve to live. Flowery rhetoric may be effective at the time of delivery even though the thought be mediocre, but that style of public speaking suffers in print. As Lincoln would say, "It doesn't scour." This is true in the case of Sargeant Prentiss. He was a whirlwind on the platform, yet his published speeches give little indication of unusual ability. On the other hand, Abraham Lincoln's speeches live, and the more we study them the grander they appear. They stand up under the test of the years. They rank the man who gave them utterance among those orators who "were not born to die."

Unlike some speakers of great reputation, Lincoln was seldom discursive; certainly not in later years, and never verbose. Instead of verbal exuberance he favored economy of speech. His style was often terse, sometimes laconic. Clay, Bryan, Ingersoll, for instance, could and did speak at length upon almost any subject and at any time;

but not so Lincoln. He was not an extemporaneous speaker. To compare the oratorical output of a Lincoln with that of a Bryan, a Clay, or a Webster, is like ranging the thin, precious volume of a Rupert Brooke alongside the lavish effusions of a Browning, a Tennyson, or a Longfellow. This son of poverty who was unacquainted with college or university won his place as a lord of language by less than half a dozen speeches of such a character as to set them apart in classic greatness. These and about the same number of immortal letters give Lincoln his place among that small and illustrious company who mastered words.

Perhaps his felicitous choice of words was never more in evidence than in that closing paragraph of his First Inaugural, which is of surpassing beauty. It was suggested by Secretary Seward, who wrote it originally as follows:

> I close. We are not, we must not be, aliens or enemies, but fellow-countrymen and brethren. Although passion has strained our bonds of affection too hardly, they must not, I am sure they will not, be broken. The mystic chords which, proceeding from so many battlefields and so many patriot graves pass through all the hearts and all the hearths in this broad continent of ours, will yet again harmonize in their ancient music, when breathed upon by the guardian angel of the nation.

The above is admirable in sentiment, but it is lumberingly expressed, and some of the words are infelicitous. For example, "too hardly" is not a pleasant sounding phrase; "harmonize" appears out of place, and "ancient music" vague. The meaning of Seward's last sentence may be clear, but the last clause, "when breathed upon by the guardian angel of the nation," seemed strained and far-fetched. Lo, what happens when a master of words takes the passage, scrutinizes it, and broods over it. It was as if a magic wand had been waved over Secretary Seward's paragraph, transforming it into enduring phrases and clothing it in ethereal beauty:

I am loath to close. We are not enemies, but friends. We must not be enemies. Though passion may have strained, it must not break our bonds of affection. The mystic chords of memory, stretching from every battlefield and patriot grave to every living heart and hearthstone all over this broad land, will yet swell the chorus of the Union, when again touched as surely they will be, by the better angels of our nature.

Here, indeed, is a specimen of English "pure and undefiled."

Biographer William E. Barton held that had Abraham Lincoln been everything else that he was and lacked oratorical power, he would never have been President of the United States. By the same sign, had it not been for his eloquence, the lustre of that presidency would have been dimmed and the literature of the nineteenth century would have suffered an irreparable loss.[2]

[2] The most engaging book on the art of public speaking in this country is *The Golden Age of American Oratory*, by Edward G. Parker, published in 1857. This valuable study opens with Henry Clay and closes with Wendell Phillips, both silver-tongued. Had the book been written a decade later, it would have included, beyond a reasonable doubt, the name of Abraham Lincoln and excerpts from his speeches, which now, like their author, belong to the ages.

Chapter XIII

Lincoln and Religion

Of all the Presidents of the United States, Lincoln was probably one of the least orthodox, yet the most religious.

—Sherwood Eddy

****

I T IS not surprising that the religion of Abraham Lincoln has been and still is a subject of absorbing interest to multitudes. "Only God is permanently interesting," says Joseph Fort Newton, and every man's relation to God is of profound significance to his associates and to himself. How natural then, that this aspect of Lincoln's character should command the interest of his biographers and of countless readers.

Nothing is more certain than that Lincoln's lineage and early environment were basically religious. The biblical names of his people prove that: Abraham, Mordecai, Levi, Solomon, and Bathsheba are in the picture. The local church, primitive and crude though it was, had a large place in the lives of Thomas and Nancy Hanks Lincoln, members of the Separate Baptists in Kentucky. The revivals were important events in which the Lincolns participated, and there is warrant for Sandburg's poetic description of the dark-haired backwoods wife singing, that summer before Abraham's birth, the revival hymns as she went about her simple household tasks. It is highly probable that the first visitors of note to the Lincoln cabin were itinerant preachers, and that the first public speaking the boy Lincoln heard was that of the Baptist and Methodist revivalists who came periodically to the community.

The place of the Bible in Lincoln's education is conceded by all who have written about him. His familiarity with the Holy Scriptures was a fact attested by much that he said and wrote. He even interlarded some of his love letters with quotations from the Book of Books. His references to Deity, prayer, and to the Savior, are too numerous to admit of disposal lightly. They are closely interwoven into the fabric of his fifty-six years.

That there were periods of his life when he was skeptical and critical of the theological tenets of Christianity, possibly flippant, is true; and this fact makes a study of his religion all the more interesting. He lived in a day when excesses of emotional evangelism and doctrinal extravagances were commonplaces of preaching and frontier religious literature. He was too honest to accept much that passed for orthodox Christian statements and creedal exactions.

However, to concede this fact requires concession also on the part of writers who stress the other side of the question, namely, his church attendance and support, together with the flowering of his personal faith in the awful years at Washington. Perhaps too much has been said of the earlier period of Mr. Lincoln's intellectual difficulties with metaphysical theology, and too little of the closing years when, on his own statement, he found prayer a practical necessity. If it is easy to make Lincoln out a skeptic, it is easier to prove him a staunch believer and Christian in all save actual church membership. The fair-minded student of his life will not wish to err on either side, but base his conclusions on both the early and later years of the great man's life. Much of the controversy on this subject is special pleading and ill-balanced in both directions. How unnecessary this kind of argument is since we have the fuller and fairer picture!

I

It is best to let Mr. Lincoln speak for himself. For instance, the charge that Mr. Lincoln was an infidel was freely made in his campaign for Congress against Peter Cartwright, whom he defeated. The following letter and "handbill," turned up by Dr. Harry E. Pratt, executive secretary of The Abraham Lincoln Association, and printed in *The Abraham Lincoln Quarterly* for March, 1942, is of absorbing interest:

Letter to Allen N. Ford, editor Illinois *Gazette*, Lacon, Illinois, August 15, 1846: [1]

Mr.—Ford:

I see in your paper of the 8th inst. a communication in relation to myself, of which it is perhaps expected of me to take some notice.

Shortly before starting on my tour through yours, and the other Northern counties of the District, I was informed by letter from Jacksonville that Mr. Cartwright was whispering the charge of infidelity against me in that quarter.—I at once wrote a contradiction of it, and sent it to my friends there, with the request that they should publish it or not, as in their discretion they might think proper, having in view the extent of the circulation of the charge, as also the extent of credence it might be receiving. They did not publish it. After my return from your part of the District, I was informed that he had been putting the same charge in circulation against me in some of the neighborhoods in our own, and one or two of the adjoining counties.—I believe nine persons out of ten had not heard the charge at all; and, in a word, its extent of circultaion was just such as to make a public notice of it appear uncalled for; while it was not entirely safe to leave it unnoticed. After some reflection, I published the little handbill, herewith enclosed, and sent it to the neighborhoods above referred to.

I have little doubt now, that to make the same charge—to slyly sow the seed in select spots—was the chief object of his mission through your part of the District, at a time when he knew I could not

[1] Courtesy *The Abraham Lincoln Quarterly*.

contradict him, either in person or by letter before the election. And from the election returns in your county, being so different from what they are in parts where Mr. Cartwright and I are both well known, I incline to the belief that he has succeeded in deceiving some honest men there.

As to Mr. Woodward, "our worthy commissioner from Henry," spoken of by your correspondent, I must say it is a little singular that he should know so much about me, while, if I ever saw *him*, or heard of him, save in the communication in your paper, I have forgotten it. If Mr. Woodward has given such assurance of my character as your correspondent asserts, I can still suppose him to be a worthy man; he many have *believed* what he said; but there is, even in that charitable view of his case, one lesson in morals which he might, not without profit, learn of even me—and that is, never to add the weight of his character to a charge against his fellow man, without *knowing* it to be true.—I believe it is an established maxim in morals that he who makes an assertion without knowing whether it is true or false, is guilty of falsehood; and the accidental truth of the assertion, does not justify or excuse him. This maxim ought to be particularly held in view, when we contemplate an attack upon the reputation of our neighbor. I suspect it will turn out that Mr. Woodward got his information in relation to me, from Mr. Cartwright; and I here aver, that he, Cartwright, never heard me utter a word in any way indicating my opinions on religious matters, in his life.

It is my wish that you give this letter, together with the accompanying handbill, a place in your paper.

Yours truly,

A. LINCOLN.

To the Voters of the Seventh Congressional District:

FELLOW CITIZENS:

A charge having got into circulation in some of the neighborhoods of this District, in substance that I am an open scoffer at Christianity, I have by the advice of some friends concluded to notice the subject in this form. That I am not a member of any Christian Church, is true; but I have never denied the truth of the Scriptures; and I have never spoken with intentional disrespect of religion in general, or of any denomination of Christians in particular. It is true that in early life I was inclined to believe in what I understand is called the "Doctrine of Necessity"—that is, that the human mind is impelled to action, or held in rest by some power, over which the mind itself has no control; I have sometimes (with one, two or three, but never publicly) tried to maintain this opinion in argument— The habit of arguing thus however, I have entirely left off for more than five years— And I add here, I have always understood this same opinion to be held by several of the Christian denominations. The foregoing, is the whole truth, briefly stated, in relation to myself upon this subject.

I do not think I could myself, be brought to support a man for office, whom I knew to be an open enemy of, and scoffer at, religion. —Leaving the higher matter of eternal consequences between him and his Maker, I still do not think any man has the right thus to insult the feelings, and injure the morals, of the community in which he may live.—If, then, I was guilty of such conduct, I should blame no man who should condemn me for it; but I do blame those, whoever they may be, who falsely put such a charge in circulation against me. July 31, 1846.

A. LINCOLN.

It would seem that a reading of this letter and the accompanying handbill should answer for all times the libel that Abraham Lincoln was an infidel. The likelihood, however, is that it will not; so perverse is the mind of man when he wants a certain thing to be so willy-nilly.

And now comes another "find" which contributes to our knowledge of the religious side of Abraham Lincoln. It has been said many times that he never became a member of any religious organization. So it was believed until at this late date (1941) William H. Townsend brought to light a document which disproves this long conceded claim.

Let Mr. Townsend tell the story:

The evidence is in the form of a large, time-stained certificate engraved on parchment, enclosed in a fine old frame of gilt and walnut, depicting the ascension of Christ, with the following inscription:

This Certifies
That His Excellency, Abraham
Lincoln, Pres't. of U. S. A.
is constituted a Life Director
of the Missionary Society of the
Methodist Episcopal Church
by the payment of One Hundred
and Fifty Dollars
E. S. Janes, President
David Terry, Secretary.

Through recent research by the writer, including examination of the Yearly Reports of the Missionary Society of the Methodist Episcopal Church, the full story of this certificate, with its history to date, may now be related for the first time.

One evening in 1863 President Lincoln heard Bishop Matthew Simpson deliver a stirring address at a Society meeting in Foundry church at Washington. At the conclusion of the services, Lincoln joined the Society, was made a life director and subscribed one hundred and fifty dollars. A warm friendship sprang up between the President and Bishop Simpson and the following year Lincoln was appointed on the board of the Society's Life Managers, which office he held at the time of his death. Bishop Simpson accompanied the President's body on its last long journey westward and delivered a touching funeral oration under the tall trees of Oak Ridge cemetery in the little town which had seen the gaunt stranger grow to fame and immortality.

II

Evidence of Mr. Lincoln's religious faith piles up particularly in the war years. In October 1863 the newspapers reported a call paid Lincoln by members of the Baltimore (old school) Presbyterian Synod. Lincoln's pastor, the Rev. Phineas Gurley, introduced the moderator, the Rev. Septimus Justin, who said the synod wished as a body to pay their respects, and that each member "belonged to the kingdom of God, and each was loyal to the government." The President's reply as reported by the Associated Press is solemnly beautiful and devout:

I can only say in this case, as in so many others, that I am profoundly grateful for the respect, given in every variety of form in which it can be given, from the religious bodies of the country. I saw, upon taking my position here, that I was going to have an Administration, if an Administration at all, of extraordinary difficulty. It was, without exception, a time of the greatest difficulty that this country ever saw. I was early brought to a living reflection that nothing in my power whatever, in others to rely upon, would succeed without the direct assistance of the Almighty—but all must fail.

I have often wished that I was a more devout man than I am. Nevertheless, amid the greatest difficulties of my Administration, when I could not see any other resort, I would place my whole reliance in God, knowing that all would go well, and that He would decide for the right.

I thank you gentlemen, in the name of the religious bodies which you represent and in the name of the Common Father, for this expression of your respect. I cannot say more.

I agree with Carl Sandburg, who in commenting on this statement, holds that there are overtones in the President's reply not to be gathered in one reading. "It was an avowal of religious faith, an implied wish that all religious organizations and their memberships could be unified for the war and a direct wish that he himself could be a more devout man than he was. Plainly it was no perfunctory address."

After many years of living with Lincoln books, talking with authorities, and pondering this aspect of his character, I am putting my own conclusion in eight counts, as follows:

1. The phraseology that Mr. Lincoln used in his speeches, correspondence, and state papers is that of the orthodox Christian. This is not saying that Mr. Lincoln was such, but that in his references to the Deity, the Scriptures, the church, and the Christ, he wrote like one. In his brief but impressive Second Inaugural, there are eight allusions to God and three quotations from the Holy Scriptures.

2. He was friendly to the church, contributed to its support, and

attended its services. In 1850 [2] the Lincolns took a pew in the First Presbyterian Church of Springfield, and they occupied it frequently till they went to Washington in 1861. While President, Mr. Lincoln attended Dr. Gurley's church, the New York Avenue Presbyterian, where he was a pewholder.

According to Henry C. Deming, Congressmon from Connecticut, when asked why he never united with a church, Mr. Lincoln answered:

> I have never united myself to any church, because I have found difficulty in giving my assent, without mental reservation, to the long, complicated statements of Christian doctrine which characterize their articles of belief and confessions of faith. When any church will inscribe over its altars, as its sole qualification for membership, the Savior's condensed statement of the substance of both law and gospel, "Thou shalt love the Lord thy God with all thy heart, and with all thy soul, and with all thy mind, and thy neighbor as thyself," that church will I join with all my heart and all my soul.

3. He was a profound and diligent student of the Scriptures; his speeches and writings abound in allusions to biblical incidents and texts. No other man in America's public life quoted so much Scripture in his public addresses as did Mr. Lincoln. His remark to his friend Joshua Speed will bear repeating: "I am profitably engaged in reading the Bible. Take all of this Book on reason that you can and the balance on faith, and you will live and die a better man."

4. He apparently was a believer in the efficacy of prayer, and was himself a prayerful man. He conceived of prayer as bringing him to the side of God and not as winning God over to his side. That he prayed often and earnestly during his career as President is so well known that it has become a platitude to speak of the Lincoln of the White House as a man of prayer.

---

[2] The date has also been given as 1849, but Dr. Barton, after substantial research, puts it 1850, and I accept his statement as correct.

5. He had a very strong and beautiful hope in immortality. In a letter written January 12, 1851, to his stepbrother, John D. Johnson, he refers feelingly to his father's approaching death, and then expressed this beautiful sentiment: "Say to him that if we could meet now it is doubtful whether it would not be more painful than pleasant, but that if it be his lot to go now, he will soon have a joyous meeting with many loved ones gone before, and where the rest of us, through the help of God, hope ere long to join them."

6. He believed in a benignant Providence, the expression of the will of One of whom he spoke and wrote feelingly as "Ruler of the Universe," "the Heavenly Father," "the Eternal God," "the Almighty Architect," "Almighty Father," "that Divine Being." His Farewell Address on leaving Springfield is so permeated with the sense of God-consciousness as to invest it with a serene and lofty light.

7. The very general impression of those who stood nearest him during the latter years of his life was that his was a devout and spiritual nature, greatly strengthened and ennobled by the Gethsemane into which his high office led him. The appraisal of close students of his life and writings is that he was singularly a man of faith. Tolstoy called Lincoln a "Christ in miniature."

8. Lincoln's mother and father were Baptists. In their Illinois days Thomas and Sarah Bush Lincoln, his second wife, took membership with a Church of the Disciples, commonly known as the Christian Church, and in the earlier days of its history nicknamed "Campbellites." His wife, formerly an Episcopalian, became a Presbyterian at Springfield, and during his residence in Washington, Matthew Simpson, the great Methodist bishop, was often his spiritual adviser. Some think that there was a Quaker strain in his ancestry, while certain aspects of Mr. Lincoln's broad and liberal interpretation of Christianity has sometimes classed him with the Unitarians. Thus it has come to pass that all of the above named communions have at one

time or another claimed him as of their faith.[3] This in itself is an extraordinary and unique tribute to a character that was simply, naturally, and beautifully religious.

No one communion can ever claim Abraham Lincoln to the exclusion of the others. He was greatly and grandly, yet withal simply, a Christian in love and tenderness. His Christianity was unique, nonsectarian, and undenominational.

With the passing years, the limitations of Abraham Lincoln's religious views, which were intellectual and technical, will grow less and less apparent, while the great basic principles of the Christian faith which found such large expression in his daily life, will grow from more to more until they quite transfigure him, if indeed they have not already done that.

[3] The story that pops up occasionally and is accepted by some as authentic, that Mr. Lincoln was baptized (immersed) privately by a minister of the Disciples of Christ communion is not credited by a single Lincoln authority of my acquaintance. See *Lincoln Lore* (Fort Wayne, Indiana: Number 675, March 16, 1942), for a discussion of this story by Dr. Louis A. Warren, a minister of the Disciples and a distinguished expert in Lincolniana.

Chapter XIV

Lincoln's Preacher Stories [1]

"Whose wit was a coonskin sack of dry tall tales."

✳✳

THE President was weary, the day had been long, and the news from the front disappointing. Mr. Lincoln sighed, stretched out his long legs, and said: "Anybody else to see me, John?"

Secretary Hay glanced at a notebook in his hand, "Yes sir, a delegation of ministers from Chicago."

"Send 'em in," said the President, and in they came, half-a-dozen strong, clad in somber black and solemn of countenance. Mr. Lincoln received them courteously, bade them be seated, and asked what it was they had in mind. The clergyman chosen to speak for his brethren went about it with a stiff formality which irked the tired man who sat loosely in his big chair.

Mr. Lincoln listened without a sign of impatience until the orac-

[1] In planning this chapter I have had the encouragement of that great Lincoln writer, Carl Sandburg. In the course of his letter Mr. Sandburg said:

"A book on your plan is not on the Lincolniana shelf as yet. It might be worthwhile to have a chapter of anecdota, the curious series of odd incidents that Lincoln told having relation to churches, church going, ministers, piety, zeal. 'I like to see a man preach as if he were fighting bees,' from Volk. The Lizard story from Herndon, with your data on the era, how it might have happened then, and the like of it as seen and heard occasionally now. The Springfield ministers who were going to 'preach down' the new Universalist fellow. And the boy working with mud, 'What, make a preacher? I ain't got mud enough.' I don't know whether these would run to a dozen or a score—and whether they would break the tonal scheme of your book. Anyhow it will be good to have as a book and I am glad this field has been covered by one of your viewpoint and thoroughness."

ular Doctor of Divinity had finished, then asked: "Doctor, if you call a sheep's tail a leg, how many legs will the sheep have?"

Surprised by such a question, and visibly taken aback, the pompous one replied: "Five."

"No, Doctor," said the President, "calling a sheep's tail a leg doesn't make it so."

There was a second or two of strained silence, then the preachers broke out with laughter, Mr. Lincoln joining. The stiffness of his callers disappeared, their business was dispatched, and they left the White House in the best of humor.

A delegation of clergymen once called on the President in reference to the appointment of army chaplains. They complained that the character of many of the chaplains was notoriously bad. Mr. Lincoln explained that the Government had nothing to do with the appointments, that the chaplains were elected by members of the regiments. The explanation did not satisfy the delegation, which continued to press for a change in policy.

Mr. Lincoln heard them through without a comment and then said: "Without any disrespect, gentlemen, I will tell you a little story. Once in Springfield I was going off on a short journey, and reached the depot a little ahead of time. Leaning against the fence outside the station was a little darky boy whom I knew, named Dick, busily digging with his toes in a mud puddle. As I came up I said, 'Dick, what are you about?' 'Making a church' said he. 'A church?' said I, 'What do you mean?' 'Why yes,' said Dick, pointing with his toe. 'Don't you see, there's the steps and there's the door; here's the pews where the folks sit, and there's the pulpit.' 'Yes, I see' said I, 'but why don't you make a minister?' 'Laws,' answered Dick with a grin, 'cause I hain't got mud enough.' "

The President once confessed to David Homer Bates in the telegraph office on the White House Lawn that his story-telling was a habit which he found hard to break. His case, Lincoln told Bates, was like that of an old colored man on a plantation who let his work slide to preach. At last he was ordered to report to the Big House, where the master scolded him and threatened hard punishment the next time he was caught preaching. Tears came to the old Negro's eyes.

"But Marsa, I jest cain't help it; I allus has to draw infruences from de Bible texts, when dey come to my haid. Doesn't you, Marsa?"

"Well Uncle, I suppose I do something of that kind myself at times, but there is one text I never could understand, and if you draw the right inference from it, I will cancel my order and let you preach to your heart's content."

"What is de text, Marsa?"

" 'The ass snuffeth up the east wind.' Now, Uncle, what inference do you draw from such a text?"

"Well, Marsa, I's neber heard dat tex' befo', but I 'spect de infruence is she gotter snuff a long time befo' she git fat."

John G. Nicolay, a secretary of the President, recalled a preacher story told by Mr. Lincoln which was extra good and ran like this: A wandering Methodist preacher tried to sell a Bible to a backwoods housewife struggling with mean surroundings and a lot of ragged children. She was polite to begin with, but resented his aggressiveness in trying to make a sale. Shouldn't every home have a Bible? Did they have a Bible in this home? The harassed housewife said of course they had a Bible. The preacher wanted to know where it was. She called the children and they organized a hunt for the missing Bible. At last one of the children dug up a few torn pages of Holy Writ. The woman took the pages and held them up in triumph. The preacher argued that this was no Bible. The woman argued it was, adding "But I had no idea we were so nearly out."

Lincoln enjoyed telling the story of an old-line Baptist preacher who stood up in the pulpit of a country meetinghouse, and in a loud voice announced his text thus: "I am the Christ whom I shall represent today." He was dressed in coarse linen pantaloons and a shirt of like material. The pants were held up by a button without the aid of suspenders, and a single button held his shirt together at the collar.

He was going good when a little blue lizard ran up his roomy trousers. Not wishing to interrupt the steady flow of his sermon, he slapped at his leg, expecting to discourage the intruder from further progress. But the little fellow kept ascending higher and higher. The thing was getting worse. The preacher loosened the important central button on the waistband of his pants, and with a kick off came that garment. Meanwhile the lizard had climbed still higher and seemed bent on exploring the upper part of the preacher's spine. With one sweep of his arm off came the tow linen shirt. The congregation sat as if dazed, then an old lady in the rear part of the room rose up, and glancing at the half-unclad, excited object in the pulpit, shouted: "If you represent Christ, then I'm done with the Bible."

Former Governor Joseph W. Fifer of Illinois loved to repeat a Lincoln story which another Illinois governor, Richard Oglesby, was willing to swear was true. A pompous clergyman came to the White House with some impossible request, bearing a stack of papers which told what a wonderful man he was. The President saw fit to refuse the request, and the rector lost his temper. In those days St. John's Church, across from the White House, was called exclusive, and when the clergyman flounced out of the President's study, mad as a wet rooster, Lincoln called after him, "Here, here, Doctor, you've forgotten your papers.'"

"Never mind my papers," shouted the angry rector, and kept going.

"Better take 'em, Doctor," said Lincoln, raising his voice. "You may need 'em to get into St. John's Church next Sunday."

In 1862-3 the Rev. Dr. McPheeters, a prominent Presbyterian, preaching in St. Louis, found the church closed by order of the general in command. A committee composed of both factions went to see the President, who listened attentively and then said:

> I can best illustrate my position in regard to your St. Louis quarrel by telling a story. A man in Illinois had a watermelon patch on which he hoped to make money enough to carry him over the year. A big hog broke through the log fence nearly every night, and the melons were gradually disappearing. At length the farmer told his son John to get out the guns and they would promptly dispose of the disturber of the melon patch. They followed the tracks to a neighboring creek, where they disappeared. They discovered them on the opposite bank and waded through. They kept on the trail a couple of hundred yards, when the tracks again went into the creek, but promptly turned up on the other side. Once more the hunters buffeted the mud, when the tracks made another dive into the creek. Out of breath and patience, the farmer said: "John, you cross over and go up on that side, and I'll keep on this side, for I believe the old fellow is on both sides."
>
> Gentlemen, that is just where I stand in regard to your controversies in St. Louis. I am on both sides. I can't allow my generals to run the churches, and I can't allow you ministers to preach rebellion. Go home, preach the gospel, stand by the Union, and don't disturb the Government any more with any of your petty quarrels.

One day Mr. Lincoln had a ministerial visitor at the White House who, he was told, wished to confer with him on a matter of some importance. The President shook hands with his visitor, and said, "I am now ready to hear what you have to say."

"O bless you sir," replied the clergyman, "I have nothing special to say. I merely called to pay my respects to you, and, as one of the millions, to assure you of my hearty sympathy and support."

"My dear sir," said the President, rising promptly, his face showing instant relief, and with both hands grasping that of his visitor, "I am very glad to see you; indeed I had thought you had come to preach to me."

Talking to a guest in the White House reminded Mr. Lincoln of a young Universalist preacher who came to Springfield. Three ministers of orthodox churches agreed "to take turns and preach this young fellow down." It fell to the Methodist to preach the first sermon. He began by telling his large congregation how happily they were all situated in Springfield. Launching into his sermon and warming up, the Methodist shouted: "And now comes a preacher preaching a doctrine that all men will be saved. But my brethren let us hope for better things."

General James Grant Wilson was fond of telling a story which he heard Mr. Lincoln relate. There was a southern Illinois preacher who in the course of his sermon asserted that the Savior was the only perfect man who had ever appeared in this world; also that there was no record in the Bible or elsewhere of any perfect woman having lived on the earth, whereupon there arose in the rear of the church a persecuted-looking personage, who, the parson having stopped speaking, said, "I know a perfect woman, and I've heard of her for the last six years." "Who was she?" asked the minister. "My husband's first wife," replied the woman, who appeared thankful for an opportunity to relieve her pent-up emotions.

Quite naturally the President was often exasperated by the numerous unreasonable demands made upon him. Still there must have been a twinkle in his eyes and a smile on his worn features as he replied to a delegation protesting a certain ministerial appointment.

"We have called, Mr. President," said the spokesman, "to confer with you in regard to the appointment of Mr. Shrigley, of Philadelphia, as hospital chaplain."

The President responded: "Oh, yes, gentlemen. I have sent his name to the Senate, and he will no doubt be confirmed at an early date."

One of the young men replied: "We have not come to ask for the appointment, but to solicit you to withdraw the nomination."

"Ah!" said Lincoln, "that alters the case; but on what grounds do you wish the nomination withdrawn?"

The answer was: "Mr. Shrigley is not sound in his theological opinions."

The President inquired: "On what question is the gentleman unsound?"

"He does not believe in endless punishment; not only so, sir, but he believes that even the rebels themselves will be finally saved."

"Is that so?" inquired the President.

The members of the committee responded, "yes, yes."

"Well, gentlemen, if that be so, and there is any way under Heaven whereby the rebels can be saved, then, for God's sake and their sakes, let the man be appointed."

The Rev. Mr. Shrigley was appointed, and served until the close of the war.

To a reporter who wanted to know if Mr. Lincoln intended to run for a second term, he said:

"That question reminds me of old Jesse DuBois back in Springfield. Seems like a meek little walking corpse of a preacher came to Jesse one day and said he wanted to rent a hall for a series of lectures.

" 'You can't rent a hall in this town,' said Jesse, 'till we know who you are and what you propose to preach about.'

" 'My subject,' said the preacher, with an icy look in his eye, 'shall be the Second Coming of our Lord.'

" 'Then you're wasting your time,' said Jesse, 'if the Lord had been to this town he knows better than to come back a second time.' "

The Lincoln story which follows, while it did not originate with ministerial visitors at the White House, ought to be of very great value to the preacher fraternity everywhere.

"Upon one occasion," said General Fry, provost marshal of the War Department, "the governor of a state came to my office bristling with complaints in relation to the number of troops required from his state, the details for drafting the men, and the plan of compulsory service in general. I found it impossible to satisfy his demands, and accompanied him to the Secretary of War's office, whence after a stormy interview with Stanton, he went alone to press his ultimatum upon the highest authority. After I had waited anxiously for some hours, expecting important orders or decisions from the President, or at least a summons to the White House for explanation, the governor returned and said with a pleasant smile that he was going home by the next train, and merely dropped in en route to say good-by. Neither the business he came upon nor his interview with the President was alluded to.

"As soon as I could see Lincoln, I said, 'Mr. President, I am very anxious to learn how you disposed of Governor ——. He went to your office from the War Department in a towering rage. I suppose you found it necessary to make large concessions to him, as he returned from you entirely satisfied.'

" 'Oh, no,' he replied, 'I did not concede anything. You know how that Illinois farmer managed the big log that lay in the middle of his field? To the inquiries of his neighbors, one Sunday, he announced that he had got rid of the big log. "Got rid of it!" said they, "how did you do it? It was too big to haul out, too knotty to split, and too wet and soggy to burn; what did you do?" "Well, now, boys," replied the farmer, "if you won't divulge the secret, I'll tell you how I got rid of it. *I ploughed around it.*" 'Now,' said Lincoln, 'don't tell anybody, but that's the way I got rid of Governor ——. *I ploughed around him,* but it took me three mortal hours to do it, and I was afraid every moment he'd see what I was at.' "

The men who were closest to Abraham Lincoln in his lifetime say his stories were not told merely to entertain. Rather, they came about naturally, suggested by an event or a circumstance, and were employed by Mr. Lincoln to illustrate a case or peg a point. Happily we have Mr. Lincoln's own explanation of his story-telling proclivities.

In the summer of '63, according to Colonel Silas W. Burt, several military friends called on the President, representing Governor Seymour of New York. As they were about to leave, one of the men, a certain major under the influence of liquor, leered at Mr. Lincoln, and slapping him on the leg, said:

"Mr. President, tell us one of your good stories," with significant emphasis on the "good." Colonel Burt reports what happened. "The President drew himself up, and turning his back as far as possible upon the major, with great dignity addressed the rest of us, saying: 'I believe I have the popular reputation of being a story-teller, but I do not deserve the name in its general sense, for it is not the story itself, but its purpose of effect that interests me. I often avoid a long and useless discussion by others, or a laborious explanation on my own part, by a short story that illustrates my point of view. So too, the sharpness of a refusal or the edge of a rebuke may be blunted by an appropriate story so as to save wounded feelings and yet serve the purpose. No, I am not simply a story-teller, but story-telling as an emollient saves me friction and distress.'"

The President's reply not only explains his reasons for the liberal use of anecdotes, but reveals also the tenderness of his nature in not wanting needlessly to offend a single human being.

Stories Mr. Lincoln told to his preacher guests, or about "gentlemen of the cloth," are found scattered all through biographies of him and in collections of anecdotes reported to have been told by him.

Mr. Lincoln's remark that when he went to church he enjoyed listening to a preacher who in his delivery resembled a man fighting bees has been widely quoted. It is likely that most of the preaching he heard in early Indiana and Illinois days was characterized by a lot of action.

There is a story of Peter Cartwright's announcing he'd answer in a sermon the doctrine of "once in grace always in grace." A vast throng greeted the eccentric revivalist in an out-of-door service. When the time came for the sermon to begin, Cartwright mounted the platform, which was beneath a big tree, and said, "I promised I'd answer those who believe that once in grace always in grace," whereupon he sprang up and grasped a branch of the tree overhead, held on for a minute, let go, dropped to the ground, and walked off. Lincoln would surely have enjoyed that pantomimic sermon of astonishing brevity.

Mr. Lincoln's cabinet didn't always relish his stories, or his reading to them the slapstick nonsense from the books of Artemus Ward. On a dark and somber day, when he had given his official family a selection from Ward and looked up to see a ring of set and unsmiling faces about him, he said: "Gentlemen, why don't you laugh? If I didn't laugh under the strain that is upon me day and night, I should go mad. And you need that medicine as well as I."

No doubt there are clergymen now as then, who would think some of the stories retold in these pages are crude and in some instances possibly irreverent. So be it, but it was Lincoln's way of easing his aching heart, and if a man would preach a better sermon, let him know the medicine of humor, and partake of it to the health of his mind and spirit, and thus learn from one who was:

A blend of mirth and sadness, of smiles and tears,
A quaint knight-errant of the pioneers.

Chapter XV

Lincoln in Stained Glass

His gaunt figure glorifies windows in five American churches.

****

IT SURELY never occurred to Abraham Lincoln that the time would come when he would appear in stained glass in a church edifice. Naturally, in his Presidential years, when he thought of his place in history, it would occur to him that there would be shrines and statues and monuments. But to be wrought into stained glass in a church window (he who had never been a formal member of any church)—how preposterous the idea!

If Lincoln were to come to life, perhaps nothing would so startle him as to learn that his tall, gaunt figure glorifies windows in five American churches,[1] and, singularly—or is it such?—these five windows are in edifices widely apart geographically, and representing four communions. Three of the windows memorialize the same event in Lincoln's life—the Emancipation Proclamation.

I

Plymouth Church, Brooklyn, made famous as the pulpit throne of Henry Ward Beecher, has a Lincoln window. It was dedicated in

[1] There is also the fourth aisle window on "State and Government," on the west wall of the Riverside Church, New York City, depicts the Emancipation Proclamation. Also, in this same church a statue of Lincoln is in the center panel of the chancel screen. It is above and to the left of the cross and the baptistry, and is one of the larger of the eighteen figures depicted in this section of the screen, which has for its general theme, "Christ, the Humanitarian."

1909, the centenary year of Mr. Lincoln's birth. It is approximately four feet eight inches wide and eleven feet six inches high. The President stands near a table in the center, and his right hand rests on the document which struck the shackles from millions of slaves. Dr. Newell Dwight Hillis was the minister of the church at that time, and in unveiling the window he said:

> Abraham Lincoln was one of God's best gifts to this Republic. He was given as a little child to the angel of Sorrow and Suffering, who planted his way with thorns, loaded him with burdens which made him strong for service and took from his arms all that he loved that he might have sympathy for the lowest slave. Today, Washington, the founder and father, and Lincoln, the emancipator of this land, stand among the mighty of the nations of the earth.

II

The second window is in St. Stanislaus Cathedral of the Polish National Catholic Church, Scranton, Pennsylvania. In 1925, when the rebuilding of this church was in progress, and on the initiative of Prime Bishop Francis Hodur, organizer and founder of the Polish National Church, "the building committee purchased Lincoln's portrait, a masterpiece of stained art glass. It is one of sixteen others that grace the interior of the edifice." The portrait of Lincoln is in full size figure, with the Emancipation Proclamation in his right hand, and with the emblem of the thirteen original states at the lower left corner. The committee purchased the window at a cost of five hundred dollars.

At the dedication of this church on June 13, 1926, Prime Bishop Hodur, referring to the Lincoln window, said: "We understand that he wasn't a church member, but his acts and deeds stamp him as one of the greatest Christians of all time."

III

The third window, appropriately, is at Springfield, Illinois, in a church which has both Lincoln and Washington in stained glass—

the Catholic Cathedral in that capital city, dedicated in 1928 at a total cost (and this includes the parochial school) of one and a half million dollars.

A description of the window at the time of its dedication stated: "The Lincoln window portrays the President interviewing Archbishop John Hughes of New York, at the beginning of the Civil War, and the giving to him of a commission to the Court of Emperor Napoleon III of France, to induce his Majesty to hold France and other European nations from following the hostile action of England, which had recognized and aided the Southern Confederacy." [2] The figure of Lincoln in this window is at the right of the observer and is partly hidden by the folds of the flag. Besides the Archbishop there is a third figure in the background in civilian clothes, which may represent one of the President's secretaries. In the background and dominating the scene is the figure of Jesus on the Cross.

The Washington window represents the Father of his Country and our first President giving to Bishop Carroll, brother of Charles Carroll, signer of the Declaration of Independence, a commission to go to Canada, to hold the Catholic French Canadians friendly to America during its battle with England for its independence. In the background is the angel of Peace.

A unique feature of these windows, which were made in America of American glass, is that they are not leaded windows, as are the church windows of the old school. These windows are built with copper and tin as the metal binders of the countless bits of colored glass which make the mosaic pictures.

IV

A fourth Lincoln window is located in historic Foundry (Methodist) Church in Washington, D.C. President Lincoln was a frequent

[2] This statement is not literally true. There were many sympathizers with the South in England, but Great Britain never officially recognized the Confederacy, thanks largely to Secretary of State Seward.

worshiper at the old Foundry Church at 14th and G, where his close friend, Bishop Matthew Simpson, preached the stirring missionary sermon that inspired Lincoln to become a member of the Missionary Society of the Methodist Church.

In the Foundry Lincoln window, under a full-length portrait of Lincoln, is a statement the Civil War President made to the Methodist bishops who called upon him: "Blessed be the Lord God who in our great trial giveth us the churches."

In the twin panel of this window is a reproduction of the certificate as life director of the Society which was issued to the President and is now in the Townsend collection.[3] It appears under a picture of the Ascending Christ.

V

I was not aware of the existence of other Lincoln windows when I began to entertain the project of a Lincoln memorial window in Central Woodward Christian Church, Detroit, a half-million-dollar edifice which we dedicated in the fall of 1928. The times were prosperous, and I felt sure that I could finance the enterprise outside the congregation. So I set out to secure a capable artist. Having learned that Mr. H. K. Herbert, an excellent Detroit craftsman, had done some impressive stained glass work for Mr. Edsel Ford, I sought him out and sketched verbally what I had in mind. I told him that I favored the picturing of Lincoln as the Emancipator striking the shackles from a slave boy, and Mr. Herbert liked the idea. In a few weeks he had completed a huge drawing, and after we had studied and criticized it together, he made some changes, and was soon at work in the much longer and more difficult process of putting Abraham Lincoln in stained glass.

There was just one man that I had in mind to deliver the dedicatory address, Dr. William E. Barton, long-time student of Lincoln, author of a dozen books and innumerable papers, pamphlets, and

[3] See Chapter XIII.

speeches on the subject. To my delight he promptly accepted the invitation to be the orator of the event, and on Sunday afternoon, June 2, 1929, the impressive ceremonies were carried out, preceded by an organ recital by Marian Van Liew, organist of Central Woodward Church, in the presence of a large audience of representative citizens. Dr. Barton was in high gear rhetorically. A master of assemblies and at home in the place, he was exceptionally felicitous and effective with his theme. A cluster of his paragraphs follow:

Lincoln in his wildest dreams never imagined he would some day be in a stained glass window, I venture. Yet we've not finished the category of saints; it's a kind of atheism to believe that God was once among men and now has departed. We believe that God guided the hand and heart of Abraham Lincoln.

We know that Lincoln as a boy made the most of the small opportunities for education that were his. He had a history of the United States and Parson Weems' biography of George Washington—an ideal library for the man that Lincoln was to be.

We know that he had the gift of eloquence. The greatest mistake he ever made was when he said in his Gettysburg address, "The world will little note, nor long remember what we say here." By grace of his eloquence the world will remember that speech when a footnote is needed to explain in what war the Battle of Gettysburg occurred.

We know that he was a man who fought through a cruel and bloody war and never hated. We know that he could be a much sterner man than the stories we have heard of him would indicate. He was kindly, but he could be firm when justice demanded it. The one time in our history when a man was hanged for engaging in the slave trade was during Lincoln's administration, and Lincoln refused to commute his sentence.

And we know that Lincoln was a deeply religious man, though he was reticent concerning his beliefs and was never one to wear his heart on his sleeve.

When he insisted on making his Emancipation Proclamation in the face of the united opposition of his cabinet, and was pressed for his reasons, he said, "I promised my God that if Lee were driven out of Pennsylvania I would free the slaves." Lincoln kept that promise to God.

A description of this window by an expert, Miss Florence Davies, art editor of the Detroit *News*, is excellent:

> The window is the work of a Detroit craftsman, H. Kay Herbert, who is responsible both for its design and execution.
>
> Mr. Herbert understands the technique of stained glass, achieving pure color of a brilliant quality, but depending very little on the use of paint. The design is conditioned upon three panels of the window, the central and larger panel depicting the figure of Lincoln, with the angels of Justice and Mercy in the smaller panels on either side. The dominating color notes of the window are the brilliant blue and red of the national colors, the two tones combined in the garment worn by Lincoln in such a way as to produce rich tones of violet, blue and amethyst.
>
> The figures shown are skillfully placed against a background of ecclesiastical architectural motifs with the American flag employed in the field of the central panel.
>
> Kneeling in front of the figure of Lincoln is a slave boy, wearing a crimson tunic, his wrist shackles broken to indicate freedom.
>
> The same note of crimson employed in the flag is repeated in the wings of the angel figures at right and left, each of which wears a mantle of blue and violet.
>
> The figures are beautifully placed in the panels, the patterns finely expressed by the lines, and the color quality distinguished by its brilliance and clarity.

The Lincoln window is eighteen feet in height and seven feet two inches in width. The use of the Stars and Stripes as background has already been commented upon. The coloring is vivid, and changes with the time of day and the brilliance of the sun. Singularly impressive is the window at sunset with twilight coming on. The vivid colors shade into subdued hues, yet continue to be arresting and of an eerie mystic quality. It would seem that the mighty character undergoes a transfiguration as the day dies, a symbol of what has actually occurred as Lincoln was gathered to the fathers and there followed in due season his apotheosis.

VI

Lincoln admirers from afar have stood with me in the sanctuary of our stately Gothic edifice to admire this window memorializing a supreme American leader. I recall again a day when Miss Ida M. Tarbell was by my side as we gazed on the Lincoln window, and that noted Lincoln biographer voiced her tribute. W. O. Stoddard, son of one of Lincoln's secretaries, has on several occasions entered the sanctuary of Central Woodward Church on weekdays, to stand before the window and muse upon its meaning.

In this connection an amusing and understandable incident is recalled. One Sunday, not a great while after the dedication of the window, a Detroit businessman, born in the South, brought his aged mother who was visiting him, to the morning worship in Central Woodward Church. She was a sturdy member of one of our churches in the deep South, and from a family which had given several sons to the Confederate cause. The usher showed mother and son to a seat well up toward the front and just opposite the window which enshrines the figure of the Emancipator.

The service had scarcely begun when the mother lurched forward in her pew and said something under her breath. "Is anything the matter mother?" whispered her son, fearing she had become ill. "O my soul! Yes!" she replied. "Look! Abe Lincoln in a church window!" At this juncture the congregation stood to sing a grand old hymn of the faith. The son gently chided his mother, "You wouldn't object to Robert E. Lee in a church window." "No, I'd love it," she replied, smiling. "Well then, mother, remember you are in the North." So it came about our aged visitor from the South, being a devout woman, was soon "lost in wonder, love and praise." At the door, after the benediction, she greeted me warmly, and the three of us blended our smiles and good wishes together as we rejoiced in the bonds of a glorious and unifying faith.

VII

Now that the Lincoln window was placed and dedicated, the thought of a companion window memorializing Washington intrigued me. It seemed feasible. Then, too, the Emancipator, in solitary grandeur, looked lonely, while the window alongside seemed waiting for the coming of the Father of his Country. I turned to Mr. Herbert again, and in many leisurely conferences we studied various portraits of Washington. We agreed that the majestic painting by Stuart was the best model for our purposes; and the artist soon had the drawing finished. The stately figure of Washington is depicted in civilian attire, with a dress sword at his side, a volume under his left arm, a quill pen in his right hand.

On Sunday, February 28, 1932, the two-hundredth anniversary of the great Virginian's birth, the Washington window [4] was dedicated by the Honorable Newton D. Baker, Secretary of War in Woodrow Wilson's cabinet. The church was packed to capacity, and participating in the program were many distinguished Detroiters. Included in the audience were a number of visitors from outside the city. An orator of parts, Mr. Baker gave an address of rare beauty, interpretative of Washington's character, and illuminated with occasional flashes of humor.

Which was the greater of these two illustrious Americans? This question has often been asked, and only one answer is warranted. They were equally great, but in different ways. They were unlike in background, training, in physical appearance and in temperament, yet alike in honor, courage, sense of duty and sacrificial leadership.

[4] The Washington and Lincoln windows cost $3000.00 each.

Chapter XVI

A Preacher Looks at Lincoln

If a cat can look at a king, the humblest
of citizens can look at a President.

✱✱✱✱✱✱✱✱✱✱✱✱✱✱✱✱✱✱✱✱✱✱✱✱✱✱✱✱✱✱✱✱✱✱✱✱✱✱

The story of Abraham Lincoln is the American epic, full of pathos, struggle, sorrow: contrasts forever fixed.

He was born in a one-room cabin in the backwoods of Kentucky and died in a tiny bedroom in a boardinghouse at the Nation's capital while President of the United States.

He never had, all told, more than a year's schooling in the most elementary subjects, yet lived to write impeccable English and to be judged by learned professors a master of purest literary style.

He grew up far removed from cultural influences and the niceties of polite society, yet wooed and won in marriage a Kentucky aristocrat and society belle, Miss Mary Todd.

He was indisposed to kill any living thing, looked with disfavor on firearms, but became by virtue of his high office the commander in chief of the Union forces in a war which resulted in half a million slain.

He was smooth-shaven for fifty-one of his fifty-six years, and grew a beard the winter before his inauguration in good-natured compliance with the suggestion of a little girl who thought the change might improve his looks.

He was an abstemious eater, not caring what he ate or how it was cooked; did not use tobacco in any form, nor liquors of any kind, yet he associated with "gluttons and wine bibbers."

He was a voracious reader as boy and young man, borrowing many a treasured volume, but never owned a library of as many as a hundred volumes, excluding his law books.

He did not unite with a church, though he was a frequent attendant and supporter; sometimes called a freethinker, he was unusually familiar with the Bible, and during his Presidency, on his own confession, was a praying man.

He was often of a melancholy mood, subject to seasons of gloom and grief, yet was as often buoyant, laughed heartily over a good joke, and told droll stories inimitably.

He loved greatly all children, and was most indulgent with his own, permitting Tad and Willie to make a playroom of his office in the White House.

He never could wear gloves with ease; formal social functions bored him, and at his first inauguration he was puzzled as to the disposal of goldheaded cane and high hat—until his great rival, Stephen A. Douglas, came to his relief.

He wrote a neat hand, devised clear and uninvolved sentences, avoided big words, never padded his speechs, was frequently laconic and pointedly brief.

He was fond of poetry, wrote verses of a homely sort, and liked best poems of a somber or pathetic appeal, as for example, "The Last Leaf" and "O Why Should the Spirit of Mortal Be Proud?"

He observed the faults and foibles of his friends and associates, but seldom commented upon their shortcomings, and never rebuked them either in public or private—for a notable instance, William H. Herndon and his intemperate habits.

He revered George Washington, admired Thomas Jefferson, idolized Henry Clay, read with avidity the speeches of Daniel Webster.

He numbered among his friends an unusually large company of

ministers of the gospel, yet when he ran for President, only three of the twenty-six ministers in Springfield voted for him.

He loved to sit with the "boys" about the stove in the village store on winter evenings, crack jokes and listen to the gossip of the neighborhood; delighted in minstrel shows, was amused by the antics of clowns and comedians, thought a traveling circus was great fun.

He had one of the best "forgetteries" of all our public men, thus he "forgot" the shabby treatment he received at the hands of Edwin M. Stanton in Cincinnati, 1855, and appointed him Secretary of War in his cabinet.

He was indifferent as to his personal attire, yet was distinctive in his choice of a high-topped hat, long-tailed coat, and a black bow tie, worn around a low, turned-down collar.

He was called by Tolstoy, "a Christ in miniature," and of him Robert G. Ingersoll said: "His is the gentlest memory of our world."

He had the rare capacity to accept both victory and defeat with equanimity, believing that neither was what it seemed to be at the time.

He was blest with two good mothers, his own and his stepmother, and it is difficult to say to which he owed the more, so much did he owe to both.

He once wrote a friend that he wanted it said by those who knew him best that he "always plucked a thistle and planted a flower wherever a flower would grow."

He was frugal, yet generous to a fault, and a better businessman than commonly believed due to his well-known disinclination to take advantage of opportunities to make "big money."

He was, in the opinion of one writer, the most religious of all our Presidents, though possibly the least orthodox.

> He built the rail pile as he built the State,
> Pouring his splendid strength through every blow,
> The conscience of him testing every stroke,
> To make the deed the measure of a man.

He loved to listen to "the still sad music of humanity," and no other occupant of the White House was a better exponent of the credo, "a man's a man for a' that," a poem he dearly loved.

He made many short speeches and only a few long ones, but with the possible exception of the Cooper Union address, one of his longest, his fame as an orator rests upon three short speeches, namely, The Farewell Address on leaving Springfield, The Gettysburg Address and The Second Inaugural.

He was gallant in his attitude toward women, enjoyed their company; and it is difficult to imagine him a bachelor and liking it.

He early became a student of government, and in the Hoosier years the contents of The Declaration of Independence, The Revised Statutes of Indiana, and The Constitution of the United States, became a part of his being.

He was in life mercilessly criticized, treacherously misrepresented, cruelly maligned, basely slandered; and in death all but deified.

He was scrupulously honest, long suffering and patient beyond most mortals, magnanimous and just, forgiving, and a stranger to hate.

He was not a demigod, but very human; he made mistakes and profited by them; he was a lover of his kind and made generous allowances for the imperfections of humanity, and because of these all-too-rare virtues he belongs to the ages.

AFTERWORD

From Abraham Lincoln I have learned much more than I can put into a single speech, or indeed, into a book. And I am still learning, still sitting at the prophet's feet. The material is inexhaustible, the field limitless, the subject enthralling.

Sometimes when the lights are low and I sit musing in my Lincoln Room, where the shelves are filled with books devoted to the life story of our "First American," and from the walls his portraits look down upon me, I dream dreams and see visions. And there are mystic moments when out of the gloaming there seems to emerge a tall, shawl-wrapped figure which fills the room. And I hear, or seem to hear, that gaunt great figure say in measured speech: "This nation under God shall have a new birth of freedom; and that government of the PEOPLE, by the PEOPLE, for the PEOPLE, shall not perish from the earth."

A Who's Who of the
Preachers in the Lincoln Story

✳✳✳✳✳✳✳✳✳✳✳✳✳✳✳✳✳✳✳✳✳✳✳✳✳✳✳✳✳✳✳✳✳✳✳✳✳✳

There follows the names of ministers, rabbis and priests who in one way or another appear in the Lincoln saga. They are listed under their denominational affiliation where that is known. While this list is not complete, it is at least representative.

BAPTIST

Rev. Russell H. Conwell, D.D.: A distinguished preacher and lecturer; minister, Baptist Temple, Philadelphia. Heard Lincoln's Cooper Union speech. Enlisted in Northern army. Conferred with Lincoln at White House. Wrote *Why Lincoln Laughed.* Delivered famous lecture "Acres of Diamonds" five thousand times, earning one million dollars which he gave to Temple Church and University.
Rev. Josiah Dodge: Preacher at Baptist Church on Nolin Creek near Lincoln farm, "a fearless expounder of the Word."
Rev. William Downs: 1782-1860. Minister at Little Mount Baptist Church near Hodgenville, Kentucky. Probably the first preacher Abraham Lincoln ever heard. An opponent of slavery, a Separate Baptist, famous for his eloquence, but careless in his habits.
Rev. David Elkins: He preached the funeral sermon for Nancy Hanks Lincoln. There is some evidence that Elkins resided in the Lincoln neighborhood when the family resided on Nolin Creek. Elkins was a man of natural ability and no formal education. He was unable to write his name, and poor in this world's goods.

Rev. E. H. Gray, D.D.: Chaplain of the United States Senate at time of Lincoln's assassination; offered closing prayer at the funeral services in the White House.

Rev. N. W. Miner: Pastor, First Baptist Church, Springfield, Illinois. Neighbor of A. Lincoln. Also served with him on board of managers of State Colonization Society. He left the testimony that Mrs. Lincoln said the last day of her husband's life was the happiest. Also that Lincoln expressed to his wife the hope that they might some day visit the Holy Land.

Rev. John Mason Peck, D.D.: A New Englander who came to Illinois in 1789, and served fruitfully as minister, educator, and editor. Lincoln regarded Dr. Peck highly, and wrote him an important letter, March 21, 1848, bearing on the Mexican War issue.

Rev. Thomas C. Teasedale: One-time minister, Baptist Church, Springfield, Missouri, who became connected with an orphans' home for the care of children whose fathers had been killed by Union soldiers. He solicited aid from Lincoln, who smiled and said: "We want you rebels into such straits that you will be willing to give up this wicked rebellion."

Preachers at Pigeon Creek Baptist Church, Spencer County, Indiana: Rev. Samuel Bristow; Rev. Jeremiah Cash; Rev. Thomas Downs, brother of William; Rev. Charles Harper, who married Lincoln's sister Sarah to Aaron Grigsby, August 2, 1826; Rev. Young LaMar; Rev. John Richardson; Rev. Adam Shoemaker—all sturdy exponents of the gospel according to the Bible as Baptists interpreted it. The youth Lincoln must have known some of these preachers and, it well may have been, all of them.

CONGREGATIONALIST

Rev. Lyman Abbott, D.D.: Successor to Henry Ward Beecher at Plymouth Church; minister of the Congregational Church in Terre Haute, Indiana, during the Civil War. In his twenty-fourth year he heard Lincoln's speech in Cooper Union, and from then to the end of his life Dr. Abbott was a student of Lincoln's life, and a devoted worshiper at that shrine of greatness.

Rev. William E. Barton, D.D., Litt.D.: One of the most prolific of writers on Lincoln, author of eleven volumes on the subject and scores of monographs, lectures, and papers, moderator National Conference Congregational Churches from 1921 to 23, editor, *The Advance,* and illustrious as preacher and pastor. His was the longest biographical sketch in *Who's Who in America,* 1930-31. Born in Illinois in 1861, died in Foxboro, Massachusetts, 1932.

Rev. Henry Ward Beecher: "The Shakespeare of the Pulpit," and internationally-known preacher, lecturer, and author. Impatient with Lincoln at first, he grew in admiration of the President. Went to England to speak for the Union Cause, and was Mr. Lincoln's choice as orator of the day when the Stars and Stripes were raised again over Fort Sumter. His address on "The Effect of the Death of Lincoln" was a finished specimen of funeral eloquence.

Rev. Thomas K. Beecher, D.D.: This unique and versatile member of the renowned Beecher family put the First Congregational Church of Elmira, New York, on the map. Thomas K. had one important conference with Lincoln during which he laid before him a conspiracy of the "Copperheads" to capture the President.

Rev. Charles Reynolds Broun, D.D.: Long-time dean of Yale Divinity School. His long disquisition on "Abraham Lincoln the Greatest Man of the Nineteenth Century" has been pronounced by competent critics as one of the finest of the myriad addresses which the centenary of Lincoln's birth inspired. High tribute this, but there is reason for it.

Rev. Charles Ellis: Minister Congregational[1] Church, Bloomington, Illinois, and an abolitionist. On Sunday, April 23rd, nine days after Mr. Lincoln's death, the Rev. Mr. Ellis bitterly assailed the policies of the late President. His remarks were indignantly repudiated by Lincoln's Bloomington friends. Jesse W. Fell, closest of these friends, defended the minister's right of free speech while deploring his lack of good taste.

Rev. Newell Dwight Hillis, D.D.: Successor to Dr. Abbott at Plymouth Church, Plymouth, brilliant pulpiteer, author and lecturer . . . a Lincoln orator of distinction.

Rev. Owen Lovejoy: Minister of the Congregational Church at Princeton, Illinois, seventeen years, and a member of Congress. Of noble mien, and a fiery abolitionist, Lovejoy supported Lincoln's policies, and was beloved by the President. An orator of distinction who spoke with passionate convictions, he did not live to see the outcome of the struggle in which he had given his all. He died in 1864.

[1] Later this liberal Congregational Church became Unitarian—and still is.

Rev. Richard S. Storrs, Jr., D.D.: Of Brooklyn, New York, a pulpit orator of Ciceronian eloquence, and a rival of Henry Ward Beecher in pulpit gifts. His oration on "President Abraham Lincoln" delivered in Brooklyn, 1865, at the request of The War Fund Committee was superb.

Rev. Julian M. Sturtevant, D.D.: New Englander who came to Illinois, founded Illinois College, Jacksonville, and taught there for fifty-six years. He served as president of that institution from 1844 to 1876. Dr. Sturtevant knew Lincoln for two decades of Illinois years, was at first critical of him politically, but came to be one of his warmest supporters.

Rev. J. P. Thompson: Minister and army chaplain. Intoned Lincoln's Second Inaugural at the memorial services for Lincoln, New York City, April 25, 1865.

DISCIPLES OF CHRIST (Christian Church)

Edward D. Baker and James A. Garfield: Although they never held regular pastorates, were members of the Disciples of Christ communion, and often preached for their churches. Baker, a United States senator from Oregon at the time, was killed at the Battle of Ball's Bluff. Lincoln named his second son for Edward D. Baker. Garfield, originally a teacher in Hiram College, and a preacher, too, turned to law, served in Congress, was a Union general in the war, was elected President of the United States, and like Lincoln, was struck down by an assassin's bullet.

Rev. Josephus Hewett: Organized the Christian Church in Springfield in 1832. Lincoln knew and loved Hewett, and wrote him from Congress in 1850 a letter couched in affectionate terms. Hewett was born in New York City, moved to Kentucky, and came to Illinois in 1832. Moved to Mississippi in 1838.

Rev. George W. Minier: A Pennsylvanian by birth, came to Illinois in 1857. A man of culture, and prominent in religious and educational circles. He knew and admired Lincoln, and never tired of writing and speaking about him. The town of Minier, Illinois, was named for this courtly Christian minister.

Rev. Benjamin H. Smith, LL.D.: Former president of Christian University, Canton, Missouri, now Culver-Stockton College. He was minister of the Christian Church in Springfield where Stephen T. Logan,

Lincoln's second law partner, was an influential member. Dr. Smith had the unique experience of preaching a sermon to Lincoln at his request behind the locked door in the latter's law office.

Rev. Louis A. Warren, Litt. D.: One of the world's leading Lincoln authors and authorities. Left the active pastorate to become Director of the Lincoln National Life Foundation. Author, *Lincoln's Parentage and Childhood.* Editor, *Lincoln Lore.* Lectures constantly on Lincoln theme, has published numerous papers and monographs of an historical nature.

EPISCOPALIAN

Rev. Albert Taylor Bledsoe: Born in Frankfort, Kentucky, 1809. Soldier, college professor, lawyer, editor and Episcopal clergyman. A mathematician of eminence, is said to have taught Lincoln, whose office adjoined, the principles of Euclid. Became a champion of Secession and sided with the Confederacy. He died in 1877 and was buried near his friend, the famous Professor William Holman McGuffey, in the cemetery of the University of Virginia, Charlottesville.

Rev. Phillips Brooks, D.D.: A bishop, and world-renowned as a powerful preacher. He was a Philadelphia rector at the time of Lincoln's assassination. His oration on the President ranks perhaps only a little below the eulogy given by Henry Ward Beecher in Brooklyn. In Brooks' diary are many items regarding Lincoln of interest to students of his life.

Rev. Charles Dresser, D.D.: Rector of the parish known in Springfield, Illinois, as St. Paul's. He officiated at the marriage of Abraham Lincoln and Mary Todd, November 4, 1842. In 1844 he sold his residence on Jackson and Eighth streets, Springfield, to the Lincolns. Dr. Dresser died in Springfield less than two months before President Lincoln's assassination and is buried on a hill not far from the Lincoln Tomb.

Rev. C. H. Hall: Rector of the Church of the Epiphany, Washington. Read the Scripture at the funeral services at the White House. He read from the Episcopal burial service the passage which begins with "I am the resurrection and the life," and then opening the Bible intoned the sonorous sentences of the fifteenth chapter of First Corinthians.

Bishop Charles P. McIlvaine, D.D.: Distinguished churchman who frequently conferred with Lincoln during his Presidency. When the funeral train bearing Lincoln's body stopped at Cleveland en route to Illinois, Bishop McIlvaine offered a prayer at the obsequies held in that city.

Rev. Joseph Fort Newton, D.D., Litt. D.: Minister of Preaching, St. James' Church, Philadelphia. Noted author, pulpit genius, and painstaking Lincoln scholar and gifted orator. He wrote *Lincoln and Herndon,* the classic on the subject. Master of a chastely beautiful literary style. Born in 1876 in Texas, and for a time minister, City Temple, London, England.

Rev. S. C. Thrall, D.D.: Rector of the Church of the Redeemer, New York. Noted for his address in Christ Church, New Orleans, April 23, 1865, on "The President's Death a National Responsibility, the President's Character a Treasury of Memory." The address was given at the request of the officers of the army and navy.

Rev. Stephan H. Tyng, D.D.: Noted rector of St. George's Church, New York City. Offered prayer at the memorial services for Lincoln at Union Square, that city, April 25, 1865.

Rev. Francis Vinton: Rector of Trinity Church, New York. Was summoned by Mrs. Lincoln to the White House to console and comfort her following the death of her son Willie. Dr. Vinton delivered a memorial sermon on President Lincoln in which he expounded a weird theology.

JEWISH

Rabbi Elkan Conn: Congregation Emanuel, San Francisco. News of Lincoln's assassination given him as he entered his pulpit April 16, 1864, he burst into tears. When he recovered from the shock, the sermon that followed was of singular panegyric beauty and tenderness.

Rabbi David Einhorn: Delivered to his congregation on April 19, 1865, in German, funeral oration which was widely quoted.

Rabbi Michael Heilprin: Offered a prayer in memory of President Lincoln which was printed in entirety in the New York *Herald,* April 20, 1865.

Rabbi Emil Hirsch, D.D.: Of Chicago, whose admiration for Lincoln found expression in a score or more of impressive sermons, lectures, and addresses. He was one of the principal orators in the huge Chicago centenary celebration in 1909.

Rabbi Nathan Krass, D.D.: Long-time spiritual leader of Temple Emanu-El, New York. Erudite scholar and popular lecturer, ardent student and eloquent interpreter of the life and labors of Abraham Lincoln.

Rabbi Isaac Leeser: Congregation Beth-El-Emeth, New York City. Pronounced eulogy on Lincoln on April 15, 1865, to his congregation.

Rabbi Max Lilienthal: His funeral address at Broadway Synagogue, April 22, 1865, remarkable for its interpretation of the character of Lincoln.

Rabbi Sabato Morais, D.D.: Congregation Mikveh Israel, Philadelphia. His loyalty to Lincoln's administration was notable. A scholar and noble citizen. Delivered impressive eulogy on Lincoln, Philadelphia, April 19, 1865.

Rabbi Max Schlessinger: His funeral oration on the President's assassination given before the Congregation Temple Ansbe Emath, Albany, New York, April 19, 1865, deserves honorable mention here.

Rabbi Isaac M. Wise, D.D.: Congregation Lodge Street Temple, Cincinnati. A learned scholar who in his sermon on Lincoln delivered April 19, 1865, claimed for the President a Jewish ancestry.

METHODIST

Rev. Peter Akers, D.D.: Contemporary and compeer of Peter Cartwright, and a preacher of parts. Lincoln enjoyed hearing Akers, and spoke of him as "the most impressive preacher I have heard," spoken, of course, in the earlier years of Lincoln's residence in Illinois. Akers was the first Methodist preacher in the state to be given the honorary degree of Doctor of Divinity, and Cartwright the second.

Bishop Edward R. Ames: Opened the school in Lebanon, Illinois, that became McKendree College. He was a devoted friend of Lincoln, an ardent Unionist, and was a welcome guest of President Lincoln in the White House on several occasions.

Rev. John S. Barger: Succeeded Colonel Jaquess as pastor of the First Methodist Church of Springfield. In a letter written to Leonard Swett, December 17, 1854, Lincoln referred to Barger as a man of might. He was one of the incorporators of McKendree College at Lebanon, Illinois, and known as "the fighting parson."

Rev. Peter Cartwright, D.D.: Famous circuit rider, "Son of Thunder," erratic, a powerful and picturesque orator. A Jacksonian Democrat, he was defeated by Lincoln in 1846 for Congress in a spirited contest. Lincoln voted for Cartwright, as the poll book shows. A maker of Illinois history, Cartwright died in 1872 and is buried in Pleasant Plains Cemetery near where he had resided since 1824.

Rev. Ervin Chapman, D.D., LL.D.: Eminent clergyman who had a government position at Washington in Lincoln's brief second administration, and was personally acquainted with the statesmen of that period. An orator of popular appeal, intensely patriotic. Dr. Chapman brought out his two-volume work in 1917, entitled *Latest Light on Abraham Lincoln*, surely a labor of love.

Rev. Newton Cloud: Served with Lincoln in the Illinois legislature, and was Speaker of the House in 1847, and a member of the Constitutional Convention of the same year. Politically he was a Democrat.

Rev. Jacob M. Early: Minister and physician of Springfield. Campaigned against Lincoln for legislature in 1836. After Early's tragic death (he was killed by a fellow townsman), Lincoln was appointed guardian *ad litem* for Early's children.

Rev. Calvin Fairbank: A half-forgotten hero of the antislavery movement. Born in New York State in 1816, of Methodist parentage, he was a graduate of Oberlin College and was ordained to the Methodist ministry. Early in his career he became a firebrand of the Abolitionists and was the means of leading some seventy slaves from Kentucky to Ohio and freedom. For this offense he served seventeen years in Frankfort, Kentucky. Pardoned by President Lincoln, he heard the President's Second Inaugural address, and attended the levee at the White House that evening. Fairbank preached in Washington before the President, his cabinet, and many senators and congressmen. In 1890, Fairbank, aged and broken, published his autobiography entitled *How the Way Was Prepared*. The book, rather carelessly written, abounds in dramatic episodes, and is a collector's item.

Bishop Charles H. Fowler: Famed for his lectures on Abraham Lincoln which he gave throughout the country. He usually spoke on this, his favorite theme, for two hours, but sometimes devoted three to his panegyric on the "Martyred President."

Rev. Jesse Head: Born in Maryland. Long-time resident of Washington County, Kentucky. Minister, cabinetmaker, justice of the peace. He performed in 1806 the marriage ceremony that united Thomas Lincoln and Nancy Hanks. The choice of Rev. Mr. Head for this office was likely one of availability rather than a close acquaintance either with Thomas Lincoln or Miss Hanks.

Rev. John Wesley Hill, D.D.: Late Chancellor, Lincoln Memorial University, Harrowgate, Tennessee, which he helped to found. Author, *Abraham Lincoln, Man of God* and *If Lincoln Were Here.* Dr. Hill lectured widely on his favorite theme, and interested many eminent Americans in the university which bears the Emancipator's name and is a center of Lincoln material and inspiration.

Rev. John Hogan: A preacher who combined business and politics with his preaching. Served in the legislature with Lincoln. Hogan was a personality, "florid of face, boisterous of manner, bold and outspoken."

Rev. James F. Jaquess: Methodist clergyman of eminence who made a good soldier of the Union and reached the rank of colonel. This soldier-preacher was of the opinion that a sermon Lincoln heard him preach had much to do with the Springfield lawyer's respect for the doctrines of Christianity.

Rev. Charles Reynolds Matheny: 1786-1839. In his home the Methodist Society of Springfield, Illinois, was organized. He served with Lincoln on the board of trustees of Springfield. Lincoln supported Matheny for clerk of Sangamon County, and his firm defended this Methodist pioneer in a lawsuit in 1838. Matheny was known far and wide for his good works.

Rev. William Nast, D.D.: "Founder of German Methodism in America," and for fifty-three years editor in Cincinnati of the German Methodist *Journal.* Lincoln wrote to Dr. Nast, October 31, 1864, thanking him for a resolution adopted by the German Methodist Conference voicing strong support of his administration. This letter, lost for years, came to light on the one hundred and twenty-eighth anniversary of Mr. Lincoln's birth. It was evidently written by John Hay and signed by the President.

Rev. George L. Rogers: Born in Virginia in 1793, he migrated to Kentucky, and on December 2, 1819, officiated at the wedding of Thomas Lincoln to his second wife, Sarah Bush Johnston. The ceremony took place at Elizabethtown, Kentucky. The Rev. Mr. Rogers lived to the great age of ninety-one.

Rev. James Shaw: Pioneer Illinois circuit rider and exhorter. He resided at Bloomington for years and died there. His recollections of

Lincoln were worth going a long way to hear, narrated with a charming simplicity.

Bishop Matthew Simpson, D.D.: Eloquent exponent of the gospel and shining light of American Methodism. Stood close to Abraham Lincoln during the war years. Lincoln looked to the Bishop for advice, and frequently sounded him out on the state of the Union. The Bishop was the eulogist who spoke impressively at the burial of Lincoln in Springfield. He was a warm friend of Secretary of War Stanton. Born in Cadiz, Ohio, June 21, 1811, died in Philadelphia, Pennsylvania, June 18, 1884.

PRESBYTERIAN

Rev. John R. Bergen, D.D.: Minister, First Presbyterian Church, Springfield, from 1828 to 1848. A sturdy character of Norwegian ancestry who left his mark on the community.

Rev. John McCutcheon Berry: Organized the Concord Church (Cumberland Presbyterian) near New Salem. He was the father of the senior partner of Berry and Lincoln, Storekeepers, New Salem.

Rev. George W. Birch: Pastor, Third Presbyterian Church, Springfield. Heard Lincoln Farewell Address on leaving his home town, and wrote a vivid description of the event.

Rev. Robert Jefferson Breckinridge, D.D.: Noted author, educator, reformer, and polemic. Minister, First Presbyterian Church, Lexington. He helped save Kentucky from siding with the Confederacy; was temporary chairman of the Baltimore Convention which nominated Lincoln for a second term, and made a speech there of national importance.

Rev. John H. Brown: A Kentuckian by birth. Served six years as successor to Dr. James Smith until ill health led to his resignation. Also served on board of managers of Illinois State Colonization Society at same time Lincoln did. His second wife was a daughter of Dr. John Todd, eminent Springfield physician, and Lincoln's friend.

Rev. Samuel D. Burchard, D.D.: This New York clergyman with a flair for epigrammatic speech was one of the noted pulpit eulogists of the martyr President, whose sermonic tribute found, along with twenty others, a place in a volume entitled *Voices From the Pulpit of New York and Brooklyn,* published in 1865. Nineteen years later, Dr. Burchard, in a brief speech while representing a group of ministers who had called on James G. Blaine at his New York hotel, coined a phrase characterizing the Democratic party as "the party of Rum, Romanism and Rebellion." That the alliterative phrase was a dominant factor in Mr. Blaine's defeat for the Presidency in a closely contested election is the judgment of historians and political writers generally.

Rev. John M. Camron: Cumberland Presbyterian. Sometime preacher at Concord Church. Highly praised by Edgar Lee Masters in his book *The Sangamon*.

Rev. Theodore Cuyler, D.D.: Illustrious pastor of Lafayette Avenue Presbyterian Church, Brooklyn, New York. Friend and ardent supporter of Lincoln. Wrote interestingly of the President in his *Recollections of a Long Life*.

Rev. Henry Martyn Field, D.D.: Editor, *The Evangelist*, and eminent churchman of his day. Heard Lincoln's address at Cooper Union and achieved a notable account as reporter of the speech. Married the heroine of Rachel Field's historical novel *All This and Heaven Too*.

Rev. Abraham H. Goodpasture: Another pioneer who preached at Concord Church, of gentle spirit and the shepherd heart.

Rev. Phineas D. Gurley, D.D.: Minister, New York Avenue Presbyterian Church, Washington. Pastor and friend of Lincoln. Conducted funeral services for William Wallace Lincoln, affectionately known as Willie, the President's third son who died in the White House, February 20, 1862. Dr. Gurley was at the President's bedside when he died, and offered prayer. He also delivered the funeral address at the services in the White House, February 17. Accompanied the funeral train to Springfield where he offered a prayer at the graveside of the late President on May 4th, twenty days after Lincoln's death.

Rev. Albert Hale: Pastor, Second Presbyterian Church, Springfield, Illinois (now Westminster). "Friend and counselor of Abraham Lincoln," much loved by Springfieldians. Also served on board of managers of Colonization Society with Lincoln.[2] Paul Angle says of Hale that "he went about doing good."

Rev. John Dietrich Long, D.D.: Born in Rajahmundra, India, 1858, came early to America. Held many eminent Presbyterian pastorates. A competent student of history and especially interested in Abraham Lincoln, his most notable work being *The Life Story of Abraham Lincoln*. In 1939 his wife and son (J. C. Long) established a me-

[2] Three other local pastors served on this board besides those already noted: Rev. S. W. Harlsey, Rev. J. Pierson, and Rev. C. W. Sears.

morial to Dr. Long in the form of cash prizes for the best sermons on Lincoln, the contest open to ministers of all denominations.

Rev. Edward Duffield Neill: A Philadelphian by birth, he was graduated from Amherst College and Andover Theological Seminary, and held several important pastorates. A chaplain in a Minnesota regiment. Dr. Neill was an assistant secretary to Presidents Lincoln and Johnson, from 1864 to 1869. A paper which he read on "The Closing Months of a Great Life" is a highly prized piece of Lincolniana. Dr. Neill closed his paper in the words of Paterculus, applying them to Lincoln: "His distinctive character was this, that he was preceded by none whom he imitated, nor did any come after him who could imitate him."

Rev. James A. Reed: Pastor, First Presbyterian Church, Springfield, from 1870 to 1888. Ardent defender of Lincoln as a Christian in all but church membership. Wrote much and engaged in controversies on Lincoln's religion.

Rev. William Henry Roberts, D.D.: Long-time state clerk of the Presbyterian General Assembly, U.S.A. As a young man member of New York Avenue Presbyterian Church, Washington, and wrote description of President Lincoln at worship.

Rev. James Smith, D.D.: Minister, First Presbyterian Church, Springfield, from 1849 to 1856. Lincoln's pastor and friend. Author of *The Christian Defense*. Appointed to U.S. Consulate, Dundee, Scotland, by President Lincoln.

Rev. Byron Sunderland, D.D.: Minister, First Presbyterian Church, Washington, D.C. Had interesting conference with Lincoln at White House. Chaplain of Senate during part of Lincoln's administration, and once prayed in Senate, "O Lord give these legislators more brains."

ROMAN CATHOLIC

Archbishop John J. Hughes: Of the Diocese of New York. A staunch foe of slavery. An ardent Union man, he supported Lincoln and his policies with undiminished zeal. He died in 1864, before victory had come to the Union forces.

Father Hugo Krebs: Pastor of the Church of the Holy Ghost, St. Louis, Missouri. He preached a notable sermon on Lincoln on April 19, 1864.

Archbishop McCloskey: Pronounced the benediction at the memorial services for the President, April 25, 1865, New York City.

Rt. Rev. Sylvester Rosecrans: Bishop of Cincinnati and brother of the Union General of that name. This prelate spoke out against slavery freely, and supported President Lincoln's policies with zest. Popular belief to the contrary, the Catholic clergy are loath to take political issues into the pulpit.

II

By way of summary and appraisal it would appear that the preachers who came into Abraham Lincoln's life fall into six groups:

FIRST. Those whom he heard and met in his boyhood and youth. For instance, Rev. William Downs and Rev. David Elkins may have left upon the backwoods boy a lasting impression; surely the latter, who preached Nancy Hanks Lincoln's funeral sermon. Doubtless, too, among the Hoosiers who stood in the puplit of the Pigeon Creek Church there may have been a preacher now and then whom the lad could not forget. In Lincoln's young manhood, if we are to accept a popular story, the Rev. Peter Akers, D.D., of Illinois, unquestionably interested and inspired him. The tribute he paid this picturesque contemporary of Cartwright is racy and engaging.

SECOND. In the New Salem days Lincoln had opportunity to listen to sermons by Rev. John McCutcheon Berry, Rev. Abraham H. Goodpasture, Rev. John Camron and others, either at camp meetings or from the pulpit of nearby churches. It was in this period that Lincoln exhibited some traces of skepticism. There was a group of Free Thinkers in the community who read with avidity Volney's *Ruins of Empire* and Thomas Paine's *Age of Reason*, and dearly loved to engage "the faithful" in heated debate. It is likely that Lincoln mingled freely with this group and had his say.

THIRD. The Springfield ministers—an arresting group! This would certainly include Rev. Josephus Hewett, Rev. John S. Barger, Rev. Francis Springer, Rev. Charles Reynolds Matheny, Rev. Jacob M. Early, Rev. Francis A. McNeil, Rev. Albert Hale, Rev. Dr. James Smith, Rev. John R. Bergen, Rev. John H. Brown, Rev. John Hogan and three or four others. Perhaps Edward D. Baker should appear in this group, although his brief preaching experience was in the past. When this "Prince Rupert of Debate" decided for the law, the pulpit lost a second Beecher.

FOURTH. The ministers who met Mr. Lincoln knew him slightly, perhaps had a letter or two from him, and after his election to the Presidency and his martyrdom, magnified their slight acquaintance out of all proportion. This is human nature. "I knew him when" is a temptation too strong for myriad human beings to resist. And this fact accounts for countless apocryphal stories, not only about Lincoln but every other celebrity who emerges from comparative obscurity into the fierce light which beats upon the great.

FIFTH. The small but distinguished company of ministers who were in Lincoln's confidence and upon whom he leaned in times of crisis. This group would include Dr. James Smith, Rev. Owen Lovejoy, Rev. Dr. Robert J. Breckinridge, Rev. Henry Ward Beecher, Bishop Matthew Simpson, Archbishop John J. Hughes, Dr. Phineas D. Gurley and possibly a few others. I cannot believe that the Rev. Charles Chiniquy, converted Catholic, rated with the preachers just mentioned, in Mr. Lincoln's estimation. Nor do I think Peter Cartwright belongs to this group. There is no evidence that this inimitable backwoods preacher who won a national reputation for his courage and eloquence influenced his great contemporary spiritually. For most of their lives the two men lived at opposite poles, politically and intellectually. Yet there is reason to believe Cartwright interested Lincoln greatly, provided him entertainment, and inspired his admiration because of Peter's oratorical gifts and odd genius.

In the election of 1860, according to Herndon, most of the preachers in the North voted for Lincoln, but in Springfield, his home town, only three out of twenty-six cast their ballot for the "prairie lawyer, master of us all." Herndon was not accurate in this statement, since a check of the poll sheets shows that nine of the twenty-six preachers were not sufficiently interested in the election to go to the polls—a melancholy fact for parsons everywhere to ponder.

Curiously, Herndon mentions in his famous biography but ten of the many preachers who personally or by their writings came into Lincoln's life. This may be characteristic of the author, or again it may be that he did not know of the existence of some of these ministers at the time he wrote his much controverted book.

SIXTH. Not all the ministers of Lincoln's day were friendly to him. Some had accepted as true the falsehood that he was an infidel. Others were suspicious of certain of his cronies of whom they had heard much that was derogatory. While Mr. Lincoln enjoyed the friendship of a number of the Springfield preachers, the majority of them as noted above voted against him or didn't vote at all in the Presidential election of 1860. John G. Nicolay, one of the President's secretaries, had this to say:

> The opposition of the Springfield clergy to his election was chiefly due to remarks about them. One careless remark I remember was widely quoted. An eminent clergyman was delivering a series of doctrinal discourses which had attracted considerable local attention. Although Lincoln was frequently invited, he would not be induced to attend them. He remarked that he wouldn't trust Brother —— to construe the statutes of Illinois and much less the laws of God; that people who knew him wouldn't trust his advice on an ordinary business transaction because they didn't consider him competent; hence he didn't see why they did so in the most important of all human affairs, the salvation of their souls. These remarks were quoted widely and misrepresented, to Lincoln's injury. In those days people were not so liberal as now and anyone who criticized a parson was considered a skeptic.

There is another clergyman, not known to Mr. Lincoln personally, to whom he owed a great deal, the Rev. Mason L. Weems. This eccentric preacher was the author of a fabulous life of George Washington, a copy of which fell into Lincoln's hands as a youth in Indiana. He pored over this much-criticized and bemeaned book; and that it influenced him for good is a fact beyond controversy. Thus in the story of *Lincoln and the Preachers* it seems appropriate to include the name of Parson Weems, whose book was one of the precious few in the possession of the youthful Abraham.

Deserving mention also in this connection is the Rev. William M. Thayer, author of *The Pioneer Boy*—an early biography of Lincoln, first published in 1863, subsequently enlarged and printed under different titles up to 1882. This book was also printed in Greek and Hawaiian and had a wide circulation. According to so able an authority as Dr. Roy P. Basler, "Thayer's book, although ninety-five per cent fiction, did for Lincoln's fame what the Rev. Mason L. Weems did for Washington's."

The preachers whom Lincoln numbered among his friends represented practically all the denominations of his day, namely, Baptists, Methodists, Episcopalians, Disciples, Presbyterians, Congregationalists, Roman Catholics, Jews, Unitarians and Quakers. Few men in American public life have been so free from religious intolerance as the man who wrote, "With malice toward none and charity for all." As one whose life has been given to the ministry of the Word and a long-time follower of the Lincoln trail, I know of no words more fitting with which to close this chapter and book than the sentiment inscribed upon the monument of Moliere:

"Nothing was wanting to his glory; he was wanting to ours."

Henry Ward Beecher's Sermon,
Preached in Plymouth Church, Brooklyn, N. Y.,

Sunday Morning, February 26, 1860,
and heard by Abraham Lincoln,
who occupied Pew No. 89

(Entered according to Act of Congress in the year 1860, by Berry, Colby & Co., in the Clerk's office of the District Court of the United States, for the District of Massachusetts.)

Text:—"As ye have therefore received Christ Jesus the Lord, so walk ye in him; rooted and built up in him, and established in the faith, as ye have been taught, abounding therein with thanksgiving. Beware lest any man spoil you through philosophy and vain deceit, after the tradition of men, after the rudiments of the world, and not after Christ. For in him dwelleth all the fullness of the Godhead bodily. And ye are complete in him, which is the head of all principality and power" (Col. 2:6-10).

The figure which is imbedded in this passage is mainly architectural. It is so, notwithstanding the term *rooted*, which is, strictly, a word derived from the orchard or the forest. But the apostle's mind worked, as intense and emotive minds often do, and concentrated upon a thought all the expressions derived from different and unlike processes, which carry the same central meaning. He is endeavoring to express Christian stability. Now in a building, the foundation, but in a tree, the root, gives this stability; and to his mind, although house and tree were unlike, they became alike, and almost the same, by this common element that was in them. His mind seized only so much of each figure as would convey this idea of immovableness.

For his figure did not overlay his thoughts as an ivy vine overlays the structure on which it grows; his ideas shone through his figures as a lamp shines through the shade that is figured for it.

Paul's was a mind that had feeling strongest, reason next, and imagination only third in rank. Hence he creates by his heart, rather than by his imagination. His conceptions and his figures are always subdued by the strength of his thought. It is thought that breaks through everywhere in his writings; and his figures are only mosses here and there creeping up the sides of the great thought rock. He glances at these figures, and catches the thing in them that carries some analogy or illustration of his train of thought, and by one undressed substantive, or one lancelike verb, pierces the whole matter to its center, and dismisses it. And so, in a single line, he condenses three or four similes. Often they are rather indicated by a single word than wrought out. Indeed, in many cases the illustration of the apostle is so subtle that it seems rather to throb in the verse like a pulse, than to lie upon the surface like raiment or ornament. His finest figures, like beauty in woman, glow in the cheek, sparkle in the eye, and are seen in the graceful inflection of the thought, and its dignified motions, rather than in the putting on of rings, or robes, or ribbons. It is made a part of the thing itself, and not something to overlay it.

In this passage there are two coordinate ideas—first, that Christ is the comprehensive power of all spiritual life in the soul. "Ye are complete in him." The context shows that this is pointed at the vain accomplishments of philosophy. "Beware lest any man spoil you through philosophy and vain deceit, after the tradition of men."

Paul does not undertake to say that natural philosophy rightly and properly so called, has no use. It was of the philosophy which prevailed in his time that he was speaking. It was during the decline and degredation of the Grecian schools of philosophy that he lived; and it was to their chatter and jargon that he alluded. He says, "You cannot make a true Christian by any use of this kind of instrumentality. Christ is the power necessary for such a work."

He also set them free from vain dependence upon the religious usages, customs and ordinances of the age. Listen to what he says in this connection:

"You being dead in your sins and the uncircumcision of your flesh, he"—that is, Christ—"hath quickened together with him, having forgiven you all trespasses; blotting out the handwriting of ordinances that was against us, which was contrary to us, and took it out of the way, nailing it to his cross; and having spoiled principalities and powers, he made a show of them openly, triumphing over them in himself"—or "in it," as it is translated. "Let no man therefore judge you in meat, or in drink, or in respect of a holy day, or of the new moon, or of the sabbath-days, which are a shadow of things to come; but the body is Christ."

The direct power of Christ upon the soul was that which was to be sought and expected as the procuring cause of Christian life. Christian religion does not ask anything as an offering to God, except the affections in a pure and noble growth. A man planted, come up, blossomed, and full of fruit, is that which God expects—not a slain bullock; not doves; not incense; not acts of reverence; not reading, nor singing, nor prayer; not fasting, nor sermons, nor the sabbath-day, or social meetings; not any religious custom, as such. None of these things are of any avail before God as a substitute for Christian living. They are the instruments by which we get the other things that God does want—namely, the graces of the soul. To offer to God the instrument of religion—its customs, ordinances, churches ser-mons, and such like—is as if a farmer should bring to his landlord a load of hoes, and spades, and harrows, and plows, instead of corn, and wheat, and fruits. These are the instruments by which you get the things that the landlord wants. He is not served by instruments in the place of crops. Or, it is as if an artist should bring his easel, and pallet, and brushes, and crude pigments, but no pictures.

Now God says, "Give me the soul pure. It is the fruit, not the instrument that he demands. Prayers, and hymns, and Bible-reading, and Sunday church-going, and all manner of instrumentation, are good if they do anything, and worthless if they do not; and if they do, bring the fruit, and not the instrument, to God.

Men sometimes stumble at this distinction between religious processes and religious results. They do not seem to understand how to discriminate between instruments or means and the religious spirit which they seek to procure by them. But every part of life ex-plains this, by analogies; and every man somewhere does understand it. It is not schools and books that constitute a man's intelligence; they promote it, but they are not the thing itself. A man may have an enormous library, and may be familiar with the books it contains;

he may have availed himself of all the advantages afforded by the schools; he may have exhausted all the processes of education; but these are instruments tending to produce education, and not education: the education is something in the man himself which he has acquired by means of these instruments.

It is not rain and sunlight that men harvest. It is the things which rain and sunlight produce that men seek and garner.

The carpenter knows the differences between his chest of tools and the work which he finishes and gets his pay for. He presents a house to a man—not saws, and chisels, and planes, and hammers.

Shoes, staff and raiment are indispensable to a journey; but shoes, staff and raiment are not a journey.

Arms and artillery are not battle; yet they are means without which there could not be battle.

And so, the apostle, seeing the servile addiction of the human mind to cling to the sense-part, the visible and external instrument by which religion is excited or cultured or helped, sets forth Christ as the only, the real efficient and living power upon the human soul.

This view does not despise old usages, customs and ordinances; but it contends that though these things, in their place, are not to be despised, nothing but Jesus Christ, a living power, exerting himself upon the soul, is to be relied upon for religious growth and perfection. This is the first idea.

The second, implied in one of those covert-words in the text, is, that Christian life, proceeding from Christ as its cause-power, is gradual, successive in stages, and fixed and permanent, first in intent, but only at length in final results.

Christ is the power of life in the soul, but Christ's method is to build—not instantly to create; it is to evolve Christian character by successive developments of growth—not to cause Christian character to spring forth miraculously.

I shall discuss this question because a great many young Christians are misled, and much injured, by false ideas of what a Christian life is, and what they should seek for; and also because there are many persons of a strong emotive and imaginative nature, who employ their own peculiar state in a despotic and oppressive manner upon Christ's young and tender scholar—and they need to be enlightened just in proportion as they are sincere and honest in their notions.

There is an idea that there is a state of what is called religion that is a whole and perfected thing, which comes to men as it were bodily, either at conversion, or at some subsequent period of sanctification. There is an idea that there is a work that covers a man's soul instantaneously with the righteousness of God, as with a garment. There is an idea that Christian character is a thing which a man takes complete from the hand of the Giver. This idea is not only false, but it is very injurious upon the minds of young Christians, and those that aspire to be Christians.

I. It is the impression of many that if there be a Divine work upon the soul, by which it is changed from death to life, from darkness to light, from bondage to freedom, from sin to holiness, it must needs be a work which is the same in all. "For, say men, with great simplicity, "it is the work of God, and of course it must be the same in all.'

This subtle error, that God works just alike always—which is the most absolute error that is conceivable—which is untrue in every part of it—is very general. It is said that if one man is born again by the Spirit of God, and another man is born again by the Spirit of God, and a third, a fifth, a tenth and a twentieth are born again by the same Spirit, they will be alike. It is said that if God makes men Christians, he will make them just the same one as the other. Because there is this universal impression in respect to the completeness and identity of all God's actions, there is an expectation, and often the most confident asseveration in argument, that if God converts men and puts his spirit in them, it must be alike in them all.

And yet, God makes the whole human family—are races alike? What is the fact? Is it not that the vast human family is grouped, and parceled, and divided endlessly, in detail, though generically they are alike? Are the members of the same stocks, races, nations or families alike? Are the members of any one community alike? Are the members of any one household alike? Is not external diversity, based upon great central unities, the Divine law? Is not diversity the genius of God's work in this world? So far from expecting that all things of the same class which come from God's hand will be alike, do we not expect exactly the reverse? Are not analogies such as to make us suppose that what he does in each man will be something characteristic and special in that man, in respect to its great outlines and features?

How is it in the animal kingdom, where God displays his style?—for God, as well as men, has a style. And as we discern the style of painters and writers in their works, so we discern the style of God in his works. It is his habit. It is called the analogy of Divine operations. You can call it what you please. Is everything, then, in the animal kingdom alike? Are the members of the same species or varieties of animals alike, or are they different?

In the vegetable kingdom is God a reproducer? There, as everywhere else, he is endless in diversity. Diversity pervades creation. It was that which led to polytheism. For so far are things separated one from another, and so diverse are they in their nature and appearance, that the simple heathen could not help attributing each to a special God or Godling. Men could not yet reach the sublimity of the idea of one being so great that these endless developments were but the symbols of the riches of his all-creating soul. It was through Christianity and its antecedent revelations that that idea was developed.

Where, then, is there the least foundation for saying that when God performs a work in the souls of men it is the same in each? The work of God in a man's soul leads him from darkness to light, from impurity to holiness, from selfishness to benevolence, and in these respects it is always the same; but in its details—in the mode of its performance, in the circumstances attending it, in the proportion of its results—it is always different. God works with as great a diversity in Christians as he does in nature. As he creates men differently, so when they are created anew in Christ Jesus he follows this original law of diversity.

II. When the soul is brought, by the power of God, into the Christian life, many think that if it be a genuine work it must be a completed work. It is thought that God finishes what he touches; and that conversion, therefore, is an absolute and instantaneous transfer from a state of sin and evil, into a state of holiness and blessedness.

Most persons are instructed contrary to this, and few persons, if questioned, would admit that they believe it; and yet, there is a popular feeling, that when a man becomes a Christian he is so changed that from being a sinner he is a holy man. To such a degree is this the case, that when a man makes a profession of religion, and enters the church, it is said of him, by way of raillery, "Oh, he has become a saint." It is supposed that a Christian cannot sin; or that if a person who professes Christianity does sin, he is guilty of insincerity verging to hypocrisy. There is not in the popular mind a recognition of the idea that a man born of God is simply sprouted of God, started of God, and is yet to go through all the steps of two growths—first, that of throwing off bad habits; second, that of developing right habits. It is apt to be the expectation of the world, both in respect to those that are Christians, and those that go from the world toward the church, that they will be perfect.

Now nothing can be more untrue than that God works completed things. I do not know but there are instances to be found in which God wills, and the thing stands instantly up according to his will; but I will say this: that the law of Divine working, so far as we are able to ascertain it, is the reverse of this. In human life, and in the natural world, perfection is evolved through stages of self-growth. This is so throughout the whole realm of life. We can conceive that the power that made the world could have made the vegetable kingdom a perfect thing. We can imagine that God might say to the sunflower, "Spring up!" and that obedient to this command the sunflower might stand up instantaneously a perfect plant. But he does not say so: he says to the sunflower seed, "Go to bed, and die!" It goes to bed and dies; and then he says, "Come forth to life again!" And then the white-faced germ begins to expand. From it, roots shoot down into the ground, and a stem rises to the surface. For weeks and weeks it is a feeble plant. For months and months it increases in size and strength; and at length it becomes a noble plant, of stalwart root and stem, and with a high, branching, and golden crowned head. All that process is required for its growth: God will not let it grow by any other.

God says to every vegetable, "Do you want to be born?" and if it does, he says, "Come forth!" And then it has to work for its life. The root has to draw nourishment from the earth, and every leaf has to suck food from the breast of the atmosphere. The sun helps, the water helps, man helps—everything is mutually helpful; but the vegetable has to work up, step by step, through various stages of growth, before it can arrive at perfection.

The same is true in animal life. Nothing is born suddenly into perfection. The egg does not split open and roll out a full-grown, broad-winged eagle. An eagle is no better than a chicken when it is first born. It has to come to maturity through a gradual course of development. At first it is helpless, and dependent on its parent for food. When at length it begins to fly, it flies timidly from point to point. It is only the final result that carries thunder in its wing and lightning in its eye.

The lion is not a lion when born. It is a little insignificant prophecy of a lion in the lion's den. It is a mere cub; and how far it is from a cub to the lion, coming up in wrath from the swelling of Jordan!

And that is not all. The lower you go in the scale of creation, the shorter is the distance between the starting point and the ending point. The things lowest down and the least valuable are born nearest perfect at the beginning; but the highest and most valuable things are born the least perfect at the beginning. The lower things are born, the higher they are to go; and you may measure the relative ranks of things by the distance between their rudimentary and their perfected state. There is the difference between the higher and the lower things that are created.

Therefore, ants hatch out ants, and never grow afterwards. They have a long period of egg-growth, and they are feeble during the first hours of their life; but they soon get nimble: they are perfect ants in a day.

Flies are absolute flies when born.

Mosquitoes, when they have got through all their little transmigrations antecedent to their birth, sail off from the pool, and are fit for conspiracies and blood in an hour. It is well for them that it is so; for they have but a short time to live, and what little they do they must do quickly!

You find that a considerable period of time is required for the colt, the calf, the lamb, and the young of other animals, to pass through the appointed stages of their growth. The nearer animals approach a cerebral development, the longer is this period, till you reach man; and when you come to him you find that the child is born the lowest thing in creation. It is but a mere sac, after all. You cannot think of a thing more absolutely devoid of everything except mere vegetable life, as it were, than a babe new-born. How much is it worth at three months? You must not estimate a child through the lens of a mother's heart: that is a telescope, and sees the child forty years long! But what is a child, absolutely, physiologically worth at three months? What at six months? A lion is able to take care of itself at this age. What at ten months? It is an extraordinary child—a paragon—if it can hold itself up by a chair. What at eleven months? A colt it fit to be turned out to pasture by the time he is as old as that. What at eighteen months? Why, it is a constant vexation of comfort? What at six years? It is not fit to be out of your sight. It cannot take care of itself at ten years. The law is behind the age; it says that a man is not a man till he is twenty-one; but all boys think they are men as soon as they are past fifteen. They are not considered responsible, however, till they have lived twenty-one years, except in the lower functions of life. And everybody knows that although some men mature quick, with these few exceptions a man does not come to the fullness of his power till he is past thirty or thirty-five years of age. More than half of a man's years are spent in coming to himself.

Now do these facts justify the popular idea that God works in the production of effects in this world like a mint—a great machine with the shape of the coin cut in the dies, so that nothing but the revolution of a wheel is required to cause dollars in quick succession to come out clinking from it? Does God produce results as nails are produced by a nail machine, from which they fly in a perfected form as fast as sparks fly on a blacksmith's anvil? The metallic results which men produce are different from the results which God produces; and the difference between man's working and God's working is in the length and successive processes of the one, and the shortness and imperfections of the other.

Nothing is more false, then, than the ideas that are current as to what is to be expected from the work of God—as if uninstrumented results were more, instead of less, indicative of Divinity than instrumented ones; as if suddenness, instantaneousness, was more a mark of Divinity than successive and time-embracing elements. It is supposed that men have to climb and toil to produce results, while God has only to put out his hand, and say, "Be!" to have the thing which he desires spring into existence. But we come nearer working in that way than God does. His operations in the vegetable kingdom, in the animal kingdom, and in the human race, are by the opposite method. It would seem as if God was carrying on processes of semicreation. It would seem as if God's nature was so vast, so vivific, so full of power, that it loved to create final results by long-continued processes. It would seem as if God delighted to make causes work out effects.

The Divine method of working in the outward world, then, is not by instantaneousness, not by striking bold results; but by progressive stages of development, as indicated by the germ, the early growth, the later growth, the final evolution of the fixed form, the blossom, the fruit.

So, also, as it is in the outward world, it is in the inward world. We should be surprised if God changed his economy at this point, and the Divine results in the soul were according to another law, and were wrought complete with instantaneousness. When we come to the Bible, we come expecting beforehand, if we come from nature, that we shall find the same great scheme of working in the one that we have found in the other—and we do. All the figures employed in the Bible indicate that the same law is operative in the works of God upon the soul, that is operative in the external world. When we are brought under the influence of God's Spirit, we are said to be born again—we are called new creatures. It is declared that we must go back and become little children.

Now we know what it is to be born. We know that a long period intervenes between our birth and our manhood. We know that nobody makes a rush to manhood almost in a moment. And, knowing these things, we can easily understand the force of these figures. We can readily see that they are intended to teach that when a man becomes a Christian, he begins back at the beginning in spiritual things.

We shall find, also, that in connection with this thing all the exhortations of the Bible are against inertness. All the expressions of husbandry, and all the processes of growth in life, are, in one place or another, employed to designate the Divine life in the soul. We are perpetually exhorted to activity, and to a constant increase of inward grace by activity. "Work out your own salvation with fear and trembling; for it is God which worketh in you both to will and to do of his good pleasure." "Grow in grace, and in the knowledge of our Lord and Saviour Jesus Christ." And so, all the way through the Bible, there are recognitions of the successive developments of the Divine Spirit in the soul. The whole process of Christian experience is evolutionary, like any other process of gradual attainment.

And that which we find taught in the text, we find exemplified by the apostles. None of them, though they felt Christ's breath, were more than beginners in the spiritual life. Long years—and in the case of Paul, forty years—were they in the field; and their lives were a perpetual illustration of this law of gradual development in Christian experience. And our own observation teaches us the same thing. We never see a man instantly born into holiness of character. I have seen men that thought they ought to be, and that tried to live as though they had been. They were full of inconsistencies; and out of this false notion grew endless mischiefs which prevented their normal and proper growth.

Christ declared that the kingdom of God, when it begins in this world, is like a grain of mustard seed, which is the smallest of all seeds, but which, when it has grown, is the biggest of all herbs. He also compared it to a little leaven which a woman took and hid in three measures of meal, till the whole was leavened. If anything is inconspicuous and silent, it is the working of leaven in the meal. No man can see it or trace it. All you know is, that you put it there; and when you go to it after it has worked, you can see its effects. And Christ says that his influence upon the human heart should set in motion causes the final result of the working of which should be perfection.

III. "But is there not afterwards," it will be asked, "another experience, which is conclusive, and which lifts a man into such a state of exaltation, that, as a kind of secondary blossoming of Christian character, all his life will be one of enjoyment, rather than one of attainment? Is there not a ripening early in the Christian life, so that the Christian's work is done, and his main business it to keep up repairs, and hold what he has got? Is there not a state of sanctification—a state of absolute liberty and spontaneity in goodness? Is there not a state of Christian perfection?"

I reply that there is a state of Christian perfection, but that it is final and heavenly. It is the completed work of God. I will not say that this final perfection of the affections and of the nature does not begin to show itself sometimes in old age, even here, as the result of a long life of discipline. I will only say this: that we are so far below what is a high and perfect Christian character that we should scarcely trust our own thoughts and feelings about it. If a person had never seen any other work of art than a signboard, he would hardly be fit to judge of the merit of the productions of such artists as Corregio and Caracci. And we are ourselves so low down in moral attainment, that it is scarcely safe for us to speculate upon what a perfect character is. I do not undertake to say that God does not, sometimes, in this world, let men rest, as it were, in the land of Beulah. I do not undertake to say that at last, when men have gone through the battle of life, having suffered, and toiled, and borne their part faithfully, there is not a glorious sunset, in which the orb is complete and round, even before it goes down. I would fain hope that there was some such experience as this. There are some who seem to our judgment to be lifted up above the sordidness of this world, in whom the old fires seem to have burned out, so that the better life triumphs over their lower nature; and we love to feel that God lets them shine a little while before they are translated to shine as the stars in glory. It, however, is to be regarded, not as a stage of ordinary Christian life, but as the result of it, that we come to sanctification. We do not come to Christ through sanctification, but we come to sanctification through the experience of life-growths. Sanctification is not a state which is wrought out by the power of God in heaven, and then sent down to clothe the soul in which it lifts itself up. Sanctification is what we mean by blossoming, in flowers; sanctification is what we mean by harvesting, in wheat; sanctification is what we mean by ripeness, in apples and peaches. When a man has gone through the appointed evolution of Divine impulses, when he has wrought out under the influence of God's Spirit a perfect character, then he may be said to be sanctified. Sanctification is the last stage of Christian growth. And though I would not be so audacious and presumptuous as to say that there are not circumstances in which men, in this world, come into a certain heavenly state which may be called sanctification, though I would not deny that there are glorious exceptions toward which the minister can point as examples, and which furnish encouragement to the Christian that is striving to attain that state; yet, I would have you understand that the word of God, the developments of the church, and an observation of the lives of men, all go to show that the Christian life begins seminally, works little by little, and goes on through various stages of growth; that sanctification is attained only as the end of a world-long process; and that when a man has attained this he is ripe for heaven. It is to be regarded, then, as the law of Christian life that we are to grow, and that we are to expect to be obliged to grow.

There are such differences in our natures, in the providences that attend us, and in our educational surroundings, that some persons live in a higher atmosphere, and find it easier to be Christians, than others.

Take several shipmasters and send them across the Atlantic. One may go across in ten days, and be a poorer navigator than any of the others, who are much longer in going across. Why? Because he goes in one of those magnificent, well-appointed steamers. It is not half so hard for him as it is for the man that goes in a packet-liner, and that is three weeks in making the passage. It takes the man that goes in a Dutch brig six weeks to make the passage, and he encounters six times as many storms and difficulties as the first man, and twice as many as the second. He, after all, lays out more skill, and displays greater seaman qualities, than either of the others. If a man goes in a row boat, he does better still; and if a man goes in a blunt scow, he performs a feat that is miraculous and incredible.

Now men are built with different sorts of bottoms. Some are clipper-built, and some are built like a Dutch brig; some are tight, and strong, and seaworthy, and some are leaky, and weak, and unseaworthy; some carry a great deal of sail and no ballast, and some carry a great deal of ballast and no sail; some have great basilar qualities, and no supernal graces, and some have these graces without the opposite qualities; some are characterized by the higher feelings, such as love, and kindness, and benevolence, and some are characterized by the lower feelings, such as vanity, and pride, and selfishness. Every man is made as he is, and he is to take his temperament and disposition, whatever they may be, and carry them to heaven. He has got to make the voyage with the vessel that he has. If it is only a raft, it is of no use for him to say, "Oh, if I had a hull!" If it is only a hull, it is of no use for him to say, "Oh, if I had a ship!" If it is only a sail-flapping ship, it is of no use for him to say, "Oh, if I had revolving wheels!" You have got what you have got, and you have got to make your voyage with that. Those that are better organized than you are, have the advantage of you; but what they gain at this end, God will require of them at the other end. It is easier for a man that is naturally benevolent to come into the spirit of love, than for a man that is naturally close and selfish. Some Christians are harder to ripen than others.

You know there are some apples that ripen in June—we call them "Juneatings"; some are not ripe till July; it is tough work to make the sap of some sweet before August; you cannot sweeten the sap of some before September; some will not ripen till the frost pierces them; and there are some that you have to carry through the winter, nursing them with heat in your parlor, before you can get their acerb sap into a saccharine state. And, as it is harder for some fruits to ripen than others, so, I repeat, it is harder for some Christians to ripen than others. Some natures are more easily brought into subjection to the Divine will than other natures.

But the question is not one of ease or difficulty. The thing to be done does not stand upon whether the work of doing it is uphill or downhill: it stands upon this—that God says to you, in your circumstances, no matter what they are, "This is your work."

When a general commands a detachment to scale a fort, break down a fortification, or take possession of a hill, it is not a question of possibility or impossibility with the man that goes. The question with him is this: "I will do it, or die in the attempt. I will beat down the bulwark, or my body shall lift it higher."

When, in a certain battle, Wellington called for volunteers to engage in an adventurous undertaking, half his army offered themselves, eager to lay down their bodies as a sacrifice for the accomplishment of the work, such was their courage and determination.

Now God puts men, in this life, into different circumstances. Some have a hard road, and some have an easy road; but every man, whether his road is easy or hard, is to travel it from beginning to end. Every man, let his condition be what it may, is to come to a final state of holiness; and he is to do it by successive developments—by evolution upon evolution, and growth upon growth. No man is suddenly born into the Christian state. There is no power which instantly changes a man from a polluted sinner into a spotless saint. There is nothing of that kind known—except in novels and biographies!

There is such a thing for all men as living in a supreme and settled purpose of religion, which is never plowed nor vexed by questions, and which makes the way of life easy, just as any concentrated and individual life always is. But there is no such fact in Christian experience as coming to a calm and restful attainment, requiring no more labor, and no more endeavor, and having no more unfolding— coming to it by a spirit-stroke. If you come to such a state as this, you have to go through certain preliminary stages of development to get to it. It can never be attained except as the result of successive steps of unfolding. It may come as the fruit of long life-culture, and then it illustrates the principle of this discourse; but it never comes like a gift of tongues in Pentecost, or by any miracle.

I think saintship in this world is a poor article—I mean saintship with a consciousness of saintship. I have seen persons that looked as near like saints as anything I could think of—though I suppose my idea of how a saint looks could hardly be relied upon as absolutely correct! At any rate, these persons could not have been a great way from being saints. They never suspected it, however, and I never told them of it. Those persons that think they are saints, are persons that nobody else thinks are—especially nobody that has to live with them. All imitations of saints are like dead waxwork. They are, compared to real saints, what those lifeless beauties in the museum, under glass cases, are to the people that walk through and look at them. Those saints that keep out of work, out of duty, out of temptation, as a means of purification, those nondescript perfect folks that we have in life—I do not like them. I think they have but one perfect trait, and that is a kind of smooth, smirking conceit. That is perfect—nothing else about them is.

That is not all. There is a law of God as immutable as the spheres, that power is a natural antagonist of deceit; and that weakness, or want of power, is almost invariably covered with tricks and deceit. I have noticed that perfect people, as lacking robustness, were invested with ten thousand ethical devices. They were more perfect than other people, not because they acted better but because they had a tact of showing that sin in such circumstances as they were placed in was not sinful. They always had a syllogism, a logical slip, which exonerated them from guilt in what they did. They always had an argument to show that no act of theirs marred or blemished the exquisiteness of their own perfection.

Now, I do not think any man will in this life come to a state of perfection. The world was not made for it. It is not the right place for perfection. You would blow away if you were perfect! As long as you are to stand on ground, in bodies that have ground in them, you have got to have certain earthly surroundings. As long as a steamer runs by steam, it has got to have the smut which is an inevitable accompaniment of steam. And as long as men sleep and eat and drink, they will be something not quite agreeable to heavenly saintship in heavenly conditions!

I have no objection to men's trying to attain saintship. The only trouble is, they stop, and think they have got it, when they are nowhere near it. I do not desire anything better than to have a perfectionism break out which shall have the effect to produce a higher and nobler religious life. It is a mistake to suppose that a man has rounded up the work of developing a Christian character, which work God has made hard enough and long enough to occupy the whole period of a man's existence in this world. I have never yet seen a man so good that there could not be a little more goodness in him.

In view, then, of this unfolding, I remark, in closing:

1. It should enlighten those out of the church as to what Christians are. You ought not to suppose, when a man has come into the Church of Christ, that he is a perfect man, or that he thinks he is perfect, or anyone near it. He is a beginner, who, for the sake of help, has come into a congregation of other beginners, that they may help each other on their journey heavenward. He does not pretend that his pride and vanity and lusts are perfectly subdued. He says, "I know I am sinful. Jesus Christ is my Physician, and I am taking his remedies, and I have come into the hospital church to be helped."

The popular idea of Christians is that they are saints in a kind of blessed church pillory, like the grim marble saints in the cathedrals in the old country. And what do you suppose a devout worshiper in a cathedral in Rheims or Milan would think, if, in the midst of his devotions, happening to cast his eye upward, he saw one of those venerable saints of the niche wink at him, and nod, and caper, and dance, and commit all manner of improprieties! What an utter shock that would be to the worshiper! How he would think that the saint was enchanted, and that the devil was in it! How he would run for priest and exorcism and holy aspersion to get rid of the imp that was haunting that saint that had stood so many ages circumspect before God and man!

Now many think, when a man has been converted, and has entered the church, that the sap has all gone out of him, and that he has become a saint in a niche; and when they see him do as other people do, and as he did before, they think he is a hypocrite, and run for the priest to get him to act as a saint ought to act in the church!

This comes from a misapprehension. Would you send a man touched with leprosy into the hospital today, and go tomorrow expecting to find him well enough to come out? Would you take a man touched with the yellow fever to the hospital in the morning, and before the going down of the sun go with your carriage to bring him away? No; you would expect that time would be required for his recovery. You would expect that he would mend gradually. And when, days and weeks having elapsed, he was convalescent, and was discharged, and came out, you would not think it strange if he was pale, and tottered as he walked, and was easily exhausted. You understand that after a man has been sick, it is a great while before he is sound and entirely well again.

And when a man, diseased, smitten all through with the leprosy of sin, goes into God's hospital, the church, and begins to take the Divine remedies, do you suppose he is to be healed in the twinkling of an eye? Moral as well as physical cure is gradual. And all you have a right to demand or expect of a professor of religion when he goes into the church, is that he shall have a sense of his imperfection, and manifest an earnest desire and a strong determination to lead a higher Christian life.

Would you criticise the child that was just beginning to walk? Would you laugh it to scorn because it tottered, and stumbled, and fell? Would you ridicule a man that had just recovered from sickness, and was climbing a hill, because he could walk but one or two steps without stopping to rest, or because he slipped and fell, plowing the soil as he fell? Would you say, "A great traveler he is! Fine work he makes of walking!"

If a man was arrogant, and said, "See what a stalwart fellow I am!" and strutted, peacock-like, and slipped into the gutter, everybody would laugh at him, and would be glad that his pride had taken such a sudden fall; but if a man was conscious of his weakness, and walked unostentatiously, nobody would ridicule him. Boys will not molest cripples.

And if a man goes into the church, and says, "I am a saint," people ought to ridicule him; but if he goes into the church saying, "God be merciful to me a sinner," and, conscious of his defection, he walks humbly before God, why should you prowl about him to find out, and make a great ado over his weaknesses and failings? It is cruel! It is unmanly!

We see, from the foregoing considerations, what a man should aim at who wishes to begin a Christian life. It is not merely outward reformation, although it includes that. The motive-power of a Christian life must be a conscious communion of the soul with Jesus Christ. Christ to the soul is what wind is to the sail, what water is to the wheel, what steam is to the engine, what sunlight is to the flower and to the growth of husbandry. But with this power that which we are to aim at is gradual successive evolution toward the completion of a Christian character is our earthly life. We are to begin and do as well as we know how, aiming, from day to day, to do something more, to push the work further forward. It is a work in which we are to undertake to carry ourselves, step by step, until at last we stand in Zion and before God.

Have any of you been waiting to have a conversion that should suddenly translate you from a state of sinfulness to a state of holiness? Have you been waiting to have the Divine power, by some miraculous event, change your nature? Or have you, in your endeavors to follow Christ's example judged yourself not to be a Christian because your life was not entirely conformed to his? That man is a Christian, who, putting his soul upon Christ, says to him, "I am willing to go to school to thee, and I will endeavor to frame my life according to thy will; I desire to become thy disciple."

Do you know what disciple means? Do you know what the word means? It means scholar, pupil. Christ called those his disciples that came to learn of him. And what is a scholar—one that knows the dictionary by heart, or one that places himself under a teacher to be instructed? A person who goes to a teacher and says, "Will you teach me Greek? I will come every day and submit myself to your directions if you will," is a Greek scholar, and yet, he does not know the alphabet of the language which he proposes to learn. He will not be a scholar six months hence, when he has made certain attainments, one whit more than he is before he begins. The moment he has made up his mind to be taught, he is a scholar.

Where a man goes into the navy as midshipman, the day he puts his name to the Articles, the day he says, "I yield myself up to be controlled by the officers"—that day he becomes a pupil. He is ungraceful in his movements, he does not know how to carry his head and shoulders properly, he has not learned to stand straight, he knows nothing about military tactics, he is raw and green; but, after all, he is a pupil.

A man says, "I mean to begin a Christian life." But *do* you mean it. Is your purpose half deep? Do you understand that to begin a Christian life is to take Jesus Christ for your schoolmaster? Do you understand that it is to take pains to know what he has to teach you, and to endeavor to learn it? Have you made up your mind that as fast as Christ wants you to learn you will try to learn? With an understanding of what it is to become a Christian, do you say, "I mean to be one?" Then you *are* one.

"But," you say, "I get mad." That has nothing to do with it. "My pride smokes like a chimney with a roaring fire under it." That has nothing to do with it. Have you undertaken to subdue your evil passions? Have you made up your mind that, God helping you, you will bring your whole disposition into conformity to the Divine will? Have you taken this as your solemn life-work? Are you conscious that you are not more resolved in purposes of worldly ambition than in this? Are you conscious that there is nothing in this life with reference to which you have a more settled determination than with reference to this: "I am willing to take Christ for my master and teacher, and I will endeavor to live in obedience to his will." Then you are a Christian. If you are sincere, attainments will follow; but the evidence of your being a Christian does not rest in attainments, any more than the length of a man's journey determines whether he is a traveler or not.

3. Those who are waiting for a completing grace that shall relieve life from all effort, watching, toil and self-denial, are waiting for a myth. Many persons pray that God would bring them into this higher state. They ought to have learned more from the interview of the woman of Samaria with Christ, when he talked with her by the well, and she found out that he was a prophet. He said to her, "If thou knewest the gift of God, and who it is that saith to thee, Give me to drink, thou wouldst have asked him, and he would have given thee living water." That was a new thought to her; and she said to herself, "It is a great burden to come here and draw water, and if this man has something that will abbreviate my toil, I will believe in him"; and so she said, "Sir, give me this water, that I thirst not, neither come here to draw."

And there are many persons that come to Christ and say, "Oh, give me sanctification"—which, interpreted, amounts to this: "Give me a spirit-shock which shall enable me to get rid of work. I am tired of waiting and watching. I want a blessed feeling which shall go with me from this time to the end of life, so that I shall not have the trouble of being a Christian."

Now if you are waiting for that, the millennial day will dawn, but you will not be in it; and the heavenly day will dawn, but you will not know it. You might as well kneel down in the spring and say, "Lord, be pleased to send a crop on this field, so that I need not have the trouble of yoking my oxen, and preparing the ground, and putting in the seed." You lazy, you indolent, you conceited, you selfish man, that wants God to exempt you from all exertion and trouble, and set you up, like an empty arbor, to be looked at all your life! He will do no such thing. He says to you, in a law Divine that speaks like an earthquake, "Work out your own salvation with fear and trembling. God works *in* you, but not *for* you. He never does your work. He works in you not only to will, but to *do*."

Therefore, those that wait for sanctification, wait in vain. There is no such thing as obtaining sanctification by waiting for it. You must obtain it by working for it, or not at all. It can only come through growth. The moment a man tastes it, he says, "Glory to God!" and before the words are out of his mouth he is before God. Sanctification and dying, I think, are the same thing.

There may be instances in which sanctification is attained in this world; but that is not the law; the ordinary process of coming to it is by working. Some men can learn a language in six months; and others who are more apt, can do it in less time. So I suppose it is in spiritual things. And those that are going faster must help those that are going slower. Those that have gained victories must be ready to run to that part of the field where the press is hard on others. Where you have been converted and helped, there are a thousand men that want your help. The power of the church does not consist in preaching alone. There are multitudes that are beyond the reach of that, who need to be administered to. There ought to be those in the church to look after such. As long as you live you will have work enough in helping those that need help.

May God give us an understanding of this manly view of living for Christ. May he bring us to realize that we are not to expect re-

pose in the sweet sensations of piety in this world; but that we are
to have the spirit of work, and to live to serve him. May he inspire
us with a willingness to endure to the end, and take our reward in
heaven.